Perfect Your
Presentations

Perfect Your Presentations

Deliver confident, high-impact performances

STEVE SHIPSIDE

**LONDON, NEW YORK,
MUNICH, MELBOURNE, DELHI**

Produced for Dorling Kindersley
by **terry jeavons**&**company**

Project Editor	Sophie Collins
Project Art Editor	Terry Jeavons
Designer	Andrew Milne
Picture Researcher	Sarah Hopper
Senior Editor	Simon Tuite
Senior Art Editor	Sara Robin
Editor	Elizabeth Watson
DTP Designer	Traci Salter
Production Controller	Stuart Masheter
Executive Managing Editor	Adèle Hayward
Managing Art Editor	Karla Jennings
Art Director	Peter Luff
Publisher	Corinne Roberts
Special Photography	Adrian Turner

First American Edition, 2007
Published in the United States by
DK Publishing, 375 Hudson Street,
New York, NY 10014

07 08 09 10   10 9 8 7 6 5 4 3 2 1

ISBN 978-0-75662-614-3

ED249

DK books are available at special discounts for bulk
purchases for sales promotions, premiums, fund-raising, or
educational use. For details, contact: DK Publishing Special
Markets, 375 Hudson Street, New York, NY 10014 or
SpecialSales@dk.com

Printed and bound in China by Leo Paper Group

Contents

1 Preparation

14 Think Positively

16 Who?, What?, and Why?

22 Look at the Location

24 Make a Relevant
Presentation

26 Research the Background

2 The Content

32 Keep It Short

34 Using Humor

36 Structure Your
Presentation

38 Opening Gambits

40 Begin at the Beginning

42 Sustain Your Pace

44 Make a Memorable Finish

46 Watch Your Timing

50 Practice Makes Perfect

3 The Presenter

54 Dress to Impress

58 Deal with Nerves

62 Anticipate Small Problems

64 Practice Stagecraft

66 Using Body Language

68 Work the Room

70 Using a Microphone

4 The Props

76 Use People as Props

78 Using Whiteboards

80 Using Flip Charts

82 Using Projectors and Slides

84 Using Pointers and Props

86 Using PowerPoint

94 Sounds and Animations

96 Use Professional Tips

5 The Audience

100 Read the Mood

102 Present in Your Role

104 Interact with Your Audience

108 Take Questions

112 Handle Hecklers

114 Take Aways

116 Make a Graceful Exit

118 Index

120 Acknowledgments

Introduction

Presentations should be the high points of your working life. They are your moment in the spotlight, your chance to shine, and an opportunity to plead your case, spread your word, and influence people.

Whether you are swaying opinions, seeking extra funds, or simply trying to put your own view across, the presentation is key to every business campaign. So why, then, do so many of these golden opportunities go to waste? *Perfect Your Presentations* looks at all of the ingredients of a truly great presentation, from the research to the content, the skills involved in presenting it, and the feedback weeks after the big day. It tells you how to conquer stage fright and reach and grip an audience; what to include—and what to omit. Whether you are a seasoned professional aiming to add polish to your presentation, or a nervous newcomer wondering how to get through it, you will find the information you need. With tips and examples drawn from some of the best presenters anywhere, this book has what

Start with an impact, and go on to impress and convince your audience

you need to add impact to informal briefings, or to add a professional gloss to a high-profile performance.

The subjects covered include research and planning, the delicate area of humor, the organization of your material, how to read an audience's mood and interact effectively with your audience, and how to disarm and deal with hecklers. It covers the stagecraft of every situation from an "unplugged" performance with nothing up your sleeve to the full bells-and-whistles additions of video and animation, as well as giving pointers on props—including PowerPoint, projectors, and even other people. Most of all, it goes beyond the simple mechanical approach of "telling people what you're going to tell them, telling them, then telling them what you told them" and considers how to best to start with an impact, convey and convince, then go out on a high note.

Assessing Your Skills

The following questions will set you thinking about many different aspects of presenting and should provoke questions, whether you are a novice or a seasoned professional. To get the most from the assessment, complete the following questionnaire before you read the book, and again afterward, honestly selecting which answers apply to you.

Before   After

1 On hearing that you have a presentation to deliver, what is your main reaction?

A How do I get out of this?
B Excellent—I'll have an audience for my talents
C Interesting—how can I benefit from this opportunity?

2 When preparing for your presentation, what is your prime concern?

A What is the most painless way of putting this together in a hurry?
B What is my message?
C How do I want to affect the audience's behavior or attitude?

3 What's the purpose of your presentation?

A I'm not sure
B To get my message across
C I don't know, but I know how to find out

4 How will you research for this presentation?

A I'll borrow from a colleague, and put extra material together on the way there
B Research won't be necessary—my presentation is already polished
C I'll research a number of sources, including my own, those of rivals, and the audience itself

	Before	After

5 **How long is your presentation?**

A I don't know
B As long as it takes to get from start to finish
C It depends—I can shorten it or extend it, depending on interest

6 **How many key points are you making?**

A As many as there are slides
B They are all key points
C No more than I can count on the fingers of one hand

7 **Could you deliver the presentation without any slides, notes, or props, if you had to?**

A The slides are the presentation—no slides, no show
B In theory; I know it by heart
C Yes, it can even be better that way

8 **How will you rehearse for this presentation?**

A I don't rehearse
B I won't—I've given it before
C A "dress rehearsal" with a mock audience

9 **Which of these best describes the structure of your presentation?**

A The slides are numbered
B I tell them what I'm going to tell them, I tell them, then I tell them what I've told them
C Begin with a bang, build up in the middle, go out on a high note

10 **Which is your ideal position during a presentation?**

A At the back of the room, controlling a slide show
B Behind a podium
C Moving around

	Before	After

11 **When you present, what do you do with your hands?**

A I've never thought about it
B They are helping to emphasize my points for me
C They are calmly folded in front of me

12 **How important is PowerPoint to you?**

A It's a lifesaver—the whole presentation
B I find it unnecessary
C I think it should be used with discretion

13 **What do you think about animations, video, and transition effects?**

A I think that they're cool
B I find them distracting
C It all depends on the time of day, the audience, and the message

14 **How do you tailor your presentations for each audience?**

A Why would I need to?
B I thank the audience by company name
C I have tailored slides and name individuals in the audience where appropriate

Grand Total

	A	**B**	**C**
Before			
After			

Analysis
Mostly As

These answers suggest a lack of confidence in your presentation skills, and a simple desire to make the experience as painless as possible. You may want to think about precisely which aspects of presentation you find most daunting, and then address each in turn. Focus on techniques that help to make presentations less intimidating, such as keeping them more informal, planning them as conversations rather than lectures, and using props. Be careful, though, that you don't hide behind your supports: be sure to stay visible.

Mostly Bs

You are confident—even enthusiastic—about your presentations. You understand that this is your chance to shine and intend to make the most of the opportunity. There is a risk, however, that you focus too much on yourself and your message, rather than on your audience. It is possible that you are interested in the technical side of how you can add impact to your presentations, but you would be best served by redirecting your focus to understanding your audience.

Mostly Cs

This reflects a sophisticated approach to presentations in which the outcome, more than the delivery, is your goal. Be careful, however, not to sacrifice yourself entirely in the process—although a good presentation is about what the audience learns, if you are unable to shine, then you are missing an important opportunity. Consider working on some of the delivery techniques illustrated in this book.

Conclusion

If this is the first time you have done this self-assessment, then bear in mind the above analysis as you read the book. Pay special attention to the areas highlighted by your responses as well as the tips and techniques—these will help you to reduce the number of "A" responses, next time around, and achieve a more balanced mixture of "B's" and "C's." After you have read the book and tried out the techniques in it, retake the quiz. If you answer honestly, you will be able to measure how you have progressed.

Preparation 1

Whether you are reading this book because you're already a veteran who wants to improve your presentations, or you're soon to give your first presentation and want to quell any nervous feelings, this chapter will help you set the scene for your performance, and ask all the necessary questions to which you need answers in order to prepare properly. It will show you how to:

- Set your goals
- Answer the three crucial questions: Who? What?, and Why?
- Make the most of your location
- Do your research thoroughly

Think Positively

Some people love presenting, seeing it as a chance to shine; the perfect platform to influence people. For many others, however, the first reaction when they hear they have to present is "How do I get out of this?"

Assess the Benefits

There is always more at stake in a presentation than its stated purpose. Give some thought to the different kinds of benefits you could enjoy as a result of a well-thought-out presentation. There may be many ways to win.

- Financial: This might include fund-raising, battling for budgets, or wooing investors.
- Converts: Whether you are selling an entire world view, a political stance, or a company policy, the presentation is the principal weapon for winning hearts and minds.
- Prestige: Whether corporate or personal image is at stake (and the two may be the same when a company is represented by an individual on stage), this is your chance to stand out and gain respect.
- Individual satisfaction: You don't have to leave the stage punching the air, but every good presentation should leave you with a feeling of pride in your performance.

Focus on why you are presenting as well as how

Benefit Personally

It's normal to be daunted by the thought of getting up and taking center stage, but if all you focus on is getting through your performance, you risk losing your audience and will miss out on an opportunity for self-promotion. To help yourself focus, start by writing down your top five goals, precisely which people you hope to impress, and what message you want them to leave with. If you don't know who those people are, then read on to learn about the Who?, What?, and Why? of presentations.

Send the Right Messages

To better understand the significance of presentations, consider instead what not presenting might say about you. By avoiding presentations, you may be sending out message such as:

→ I don't understand my own job well enough to explain it
→ I lack confidence and/or competence
→ I am not a good communicator
→ I would prefer to be passed over in favor of others
→ I would prefer not to have opportunities to meet and impress my peers in the industry

Would you say any of the above in a job interview? Would you hire anyone who did? Everyone has worried about one or more of the above points at some time, but there's no need to advertise the fact. Instead, use this book to turn your weaknesses into strengths and maximize your presentation potential.

Give Yourself Purpose

Stating your goals is important because it works in two ways. There is the practical benefit—by selecting your targets, you have taken the first step toward researching and preparing, so as best to achieve them. But there is also a simple yet powerful psychological element. Having a goal in mind means you have just made the transformation from someone thinking (probably reluctantly) about the process of the presentation into someone who is motivated by its purpose. That alone will help to make you a more purposeful presenter.

TIP Give yourself specific goals. "Looking good" is too vague; "Impressing the VP with my knowledge of rival products," however, is a clear goal.

Who?, What?, and Why?

For novices, a presentation is all about "me" and "them." For the experts, however, there is a lot more to it: they imagine themselves in the audience, looking at their own presentation from the other side of the lights.

Recognize All the Roles

Of course you know who you are, but think about who you are to the audience. Are you the expert? The opposition? The light relief? Imagine yourself sitting in the audience and think about what you represent to them. When you are clear on your own role, think about that of your audience. How much do you know about them? Try answering the following questions, each one of which should affect the way you pitch your presentation;

- How many people are there in the audience?
- What is their level in the company or organization (this applies as much at a PTA meeting at a school as at the annual meeting of a multinational company)?
- What are their values?
- What is their level of knowledge?

CASE study: Understanding All Viewpoints

Karla, a project manager with an engineering company, had difficulties in getting her teams of designers and engineers to understand each other's points of view. She decided to get them to role-play—she told them what she wanted to promise the client, then asked the designers to ask the questions that the engineers might raise, and the engineers to ask those that they thought might be posed by the designers.

• As the design team struggled to understand the practical aspects of the product, and the engineers tried to correct the creative design, both teams gained useful insights into the other's function and their point of view.

• Karla learned that an exercise in lateral thinking can bring people together, as she listened to the exchange of opinions and watched her staff coming to an understanding of their real roles.

- What is their level of interest?
- Why do they think they are there?
- What do they think you are there for?

Get the Inside Information

If you don't know the answers to these questions, you should try to find out. An exchange of short emails or a simple phone call will pay dividends in making your presentation more relevant for everyone. One of the quickest ways to get an insight into a company (including your own) is to take a look at the company website. It will usually feature shareholder information, press releases, and possibly even profiles of key staff. It will probably also have a "mission statement" encapsulating what the company's official goal or ethos is meant to be. Be aware that this statement may well be news to most people actually working in the company, but it will usually raise a wry grin and help you get an insider's view of how the company perceives itself and its aims.

TIP Single out key attendees and fine-tune your presentation to appeal to them.

Ask the Question "Why?"

All too often, the reason that an audience and a presenter come together is because they were told to. Nobody on either side has thought any further than that. In fact, there may be many reasons for a presentation and the "why?" will impact seriously on the "what?" when it comes to selecting your presentation material. If you are the star attraction, then you already know why you're presenting and have probably delivered your message before. That doesn't mean you can just deliver the same speech word for word—it's still worth looking through the "why?' questions to see if anything has changed since last time.

Be Original

Even stars have to share the billing sometimes, however, and that's when asking "why?' can really save the day. Fashionable celebrities don't turn up to a big event without discreetly checking that their friends and rivals won't be wearing the same outfit. Likewise, the

Make a Connection Remember that it's the connection you form with your audience that makes you a good, or even a great, presenter.

Understand Your Role

Before you can prepare your presentation and tailor it to fit the audience you will be addressing, there are a number of questions you need to ask yourself about your role:

→ Am I here to change a perception?

→ Am I launching a call to action?

→ What do I hope to inspire the audience to do?

→ Am I providing an information update?

→ Am I entertainment rather than education?

→ Am I here to challenge someone else's view?

→ Am I here to justify my (company's) position?

→ Am I a foil for someone else's presentation?

→ Am I a substitute or time-filler?

→ How do I relate to the other people presenting?

If you aren't the star and there is no set role expected of you, you are free to relax and present yourself in your best light.

polished presenter doesn't just check when he or she is presenting; they check who comes before and after, and finds out (or at least makes an intelligent guess) what is the "why?" for each of those presentations. If your subject or theme overlaps and you are first on stage, then there is no problem. If you are the second presenter dealing with the same subject or call to action, however, it is critical to know the approach of your predecessor in advance. If it's not different enough, your message will simply blend in with theirs and end up being forgotten.

The audience only pays attention as long as you know where you are going.

Philip Crosby

Ask the Question "What?"

If you've answered the "who?" and "why?" then you're already three-quarters of the way to knowing the "what": the ingredients your presentation must include. If the "why?" of your presentation is education, take a look at your answers to the "who?" question before pulling together the information that is relevant to the level of your audience. Don't forget that even the sharpest audience will struggle to remember more than three or four key points in a single presentation. If the "why?" is essentially about selling, then by all means collect together your information, but remember that the benefits of your pitch come before any factual details.

Match Up "Who" with "Why"?

Go back to your "who?" questions and work out what content will appeal to those people. If the "why?" is entertainment, or as a warm up to another speaker, you will need to tone down the amount of information and concentrate instead on anecdote, humor, or relevant audio-visual aids to brighten up your performance. If there is no "why?" because you are making up numbers or filling a vacant slot, go back to the "who?" question and ask yourself what there could be in it for you, and how best to achieve it. When there is no fixed agenda, the stage is yours for you to pick an appropriate agenda of your own. Bear in mind that even if your own principal objective is to show yourself off, you still have to massage the message so that it interests and engages your audience.

5 minute FIX

If you have no choice but to borrow a colleague's presentation:

- Double-check to ensure your audience hasn't seen it before.

- Make sure you really do know what's in it.

- Customize it with care to include as much of your own material as you possibly can.

CASE study: Adapting to an Audience

Ramón, a technology expert presenting to an audience of journalists, turned up with a 67-slide presentation on the significance of the new service being offered. The same presentation served him well internally for staff who were new to the subject. The journalists, though, were not a captive audience like Ramón's in-house colleagues, and had yet to be convinced that the service was of any interest. They wanted an instant understanding of what was exciting and new about it. Quickly realizing that the "why?"

for this audience was dramatically different, Ramón switched off the projector, left the stage, and sat among them to explain in simple terms why he thought it mattered.

• *For the audience, changing the presentation mid-flow made a statement that Ramón was intent on meeting their needs.*
• *Ramón learned that, however good a presentation, it won't be suitable for every audience. The audience appreciated the effort he was making and listened carefully to what he had to say.*

Do Your Own Homework

Reluctant presenters are often tempted to borrow a colleague's presentation. This may seem to make sense on many levels; it works for them, so it will work for you, your reasoning goes—and it saves doing your own homework. Resist that temptation. Someone else's presentation will have someone else's answers to the "who?," "why?," and "what?". At best you will end up as a pale shadow of that other person—a corporate clone. At worst, you will miss your target altogether and end up losing the plot because you can't remember how one point leads to the next. By all means share slides, data, and anecdotes with your colleagues, but be sure to drop them into your own presentation structure and add your own individual touches. Never use the presentation verbatim.

TIP **If someone else pulled out of presenting, find out why before you agree to replace them.**

Look at the Location

A little advance research into the venue will pay off handsomely, not least by ensuring that you and your audience turn up at the same spot, and that you will walk into the room knowing it is set up for your needs.

Do Your Research

Familiarity breeds contempt, and if the location for your presentation is the office down the hall, then you will probably spend less time researching it than you would an auditorium in a foreign city. This is probably why so many in-house presenters end up perched at the wrong end of a table (the end that turned out to be near the room's only electrical outlet), while a huddle of senior executives cluster around the door where they are repeatedly disrupted by late arrivals.

Check Your Venue

No matter how well you think you know the venue for a presentation, take the time to go there beforehand and check out some of the key features. Your checklist should include:

→ Where are the electrical outlets?
→ Is there a flip chart/whiteboard/blackboard?
→ Is there enough seating?
→ Is there air conditioning?
→ Is there a phone? If so, can you make sure it doesn't ring?
→ Will any latecomers walk into the front of the presentation?
→ If using a projector, can the room be darkened?
→ Do you know exactly how to get there?
→ Does your audience?
→ Could anything confuse them? Could a map help them?

Visit the Venue If it is at all feasible to pay a visit to the venue before you present, do so. It will help you to spot the advantages or drawbacks it offers.

Be Confident You Can Cope

Imagine that the location in which you're presenting is changed at the last minute to a different room or building. Are you confident you would still have all you need to present? Think for a minute what you would do if the room couldn't be darkened for a slideshow, or if the electrical outlets turned out to be dead. Try to imagine giving the presentation in an informal setting—around a restaurant table, for example. Knowing that you have a fall-back position, and can deliver your presentation without aids, is a good way to build your own confidence, so that you are able to deal with any problems that arise.

TIP A lot of presentations take place in chain hotels. Call ahead and make sure you're planning on going to the right one.

Make a Relevant Presentation

For you to get what you want from a presentation, the audience must get what they want. Good presenters, like good salespeople, first find out what their customers want, and then give it to them.

Offer Incentives

Sometimes there is the twist that the "customers" first need to be told that they want what's being offered, but the principle remains the same: if you want someone to pay attention, you must make it clear what the advantages for them will be. Go back to the "who?" questions earlier in this chapter and think about who the key target individuals or groups in your audience are. Now try to imagine what they are most anxious to achieve, change, or resolve. Go back to your draft presentation and go through it, thinking about which point is going to satisfy which concern for those people. Be specific. You may be showcasing a fabulous new service or product, but remember that the "what's in it for me?" factor will not be the same for potential investors, for example, as it is for potential users. If you find that you can't match up the audience needs with your points, you need to go back to the drawing board and work out some ways in which they can be brought closer together.

Building Interest

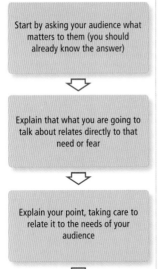

Start by asking your audience what matters to them (you should already know the answer)

⬇

Explain that what you are going to talk about relates directly to that need or fear

⬇

Explain your point, taking care to relate it to the needs of your audience

⬇

Conclude by telling them that what they now know brings them one step closer to achieving the goal they started with

Address the Audience's Fears

There are many factors that motivate human behavior, but a cynical yet accurate generalization can reduce a lot of them down to two closely related drives: fear and greed.

Fears usually divide into two groups: those that people hold for their business and company, and those they hold for themselves. The "greed" aspect is the other side of the same coin—the idea that through better information, they will outpace their competitors and get the edge over their competition. These are the factors to consider if you want to have audiences absorbed in what you say. You do not have to refer directly to either fear or greed when you are presenting—it will be better if you don't—but an awareness of them will give your presentation added edge.

General versus Personal Fears

GENERAL FEARS

- Fear that failing to spot a new market trend could lead to the company falling behind and losing out to the competition.
- Fear that rivals are better informed than you are, and will be able to perform better because of their better and broader knowledge.
- Fear that a failure to address an inefficiency will cost the company money and make it unviable.

PERSONAL FEARS

- Fear that failing to stay up to date personally with current trends will mean that ambitious colleagues surpass you.
- Fear that if you fall behind in industry knowledge, you will not be able to make the necessary effective arguments for your departmental budget.
- Fear that if you don't attend every meeting, you won't be able to justify your expenses.

TIP Everyone is both anxious and excited about their future. Learn to predict it for them and you are certain of a rapt audience.

Research the Background

Important as it is to know your stuff, a good presenter goes further and checks the background. Having an impressive knowledge of your audience's business turns an adequate presentation into an outstanding one.

Know Your Material

Make sure you have your own facts straight if you are going to quote dates, numbers, or events. Figures often date fast, so go back to the source just before you present and see if there is a newer version.

If you are sharing a stage with colleagues, ask them what they are presenting on. Don't presume you know from the title of the presentation or because you have seen them present before—they may also be reading this book and refreshing their presentations! If your fellow presenters are from other companies, give them a call and explain that you are interested in their presentation because you want to ensure you don't overlap. Ask around your own colleagues to see if anyone has seen these people present before.

Even a familiar subject should be researched fresh each time

think
SMART

Even when you have all the facts, remember to be ready to back them up in order to make your presentation really impressive

Time may be limited, but if you lead with a figure, be ready to explain exactly why it is bigger/smaller/faster/cheaper than ever before. Equally, be prepared to say by how much something is bigger/more expensive/heavier. It's not enough to know yourself—your audience must know that you know.

Know Your Audience's Business

Make a point of finding out which companies and individuals you will be talking to. Find out what their areas of interest are, what they're looking to expand into, and how well (or poorly) they are doing. Nobody works in a vacuum, and a lot of information—particularly that within your own industry—is usually quite easy to come by, so take a look at the competitors of the companies to which you are presenting, as well as the companies themselves, and see if they have anything to tell you that will help. If your presentation is part of a conference, there will be an organizer with a list of attendees, and a reason why each one is there—and this will be a shortcut to a good deal of what you want to know. Ask to see it. Find out about key individuals by asking around or even by talking to them directly. At the least, this will give you a point of contact in the audience which you can use to your advantage.

Look for the "So What?" Factor

Make sure you know why your audience will care about the points you are making.

For every statement of fact in your presentation, imagine someone saying "so what?"

Think how you will explain why you thought it was important enough to include

Clarify why that "so what?" factor applies to their business

If you can't answer the "so what?" question, consider dropping that point altogether

Information at Your Fingertips

The Internet is a phenomenal source of information for presentations, whether you're looking for facts, anecdotes, humor, pictures, or even sound and video.

Company websites are the first place to look for announcements, including shareholder information, news releases, and product catalogs, but there are a host of other sites as well. Finding out what a company chooses to say about itself, and comparing that with press coverage, is a rich seam of material for presentations.

→ Make sure you check the dates on material you plan to use. Because the Web features material dating back over years, you need to ensure that it is current.

→ Trade journals often have online versions with searchable archives that can reveal fascinating snippets about industries and companies.

→ Putting key search words into Google (www.google.com) will point you to recent news items in other publications, to help to broaden your perspective.

Most of the major business publications also have their own websites, but some archived items require a subscription. If you come across an item of interest but don't want to subscribe right now, select some key words from the subject and try searching other journals for them—you may find at least a free outline of the information. Good places to start include:

→ The Economist—www.economist.com

→ Forbes—www.forbes.com

→ Fortune—www.fortune.com

Information is the oxygen of the modern age.
It seeps through the walls topped by barbed wire.
It wafts across the electrified borders.

Ronald Reagan

Look around You

The richest and least-used source of vital information for presentations is other people, both those around you and those in your audience. In your own office or within your network of friends and acquaintances, there is a vast amount of experience of presentations—good and bad— as well as some in-depth knowledge of your audience and rivals. Most people like to talk about themselves, so why not find those who have presented before, or seen your rivals present, and offer to buy them a coffee in return for five minutes of their wisdom?

Find the Specialists

Does your industry have a trade title—a magazine or newspaper exclusively devoted to your business? If it does, call and see if there is someone who specializes in your field. They may be able to share invaluable insights about your potential audience; even if they don't, simply dropping their name will assure that you capture the attention of the audience.

Inform Yourself in Advance Go straight to source for your information, whether that means seeking out and interviewing the experts or doing thorough research into your subject.

The 2
Content

Not only is the content the meat of your presentation, it can also make all the difference to your performance, and to whether you look forward to your moment in the spotlight. If your content is well chosen, structured, and timed, you will have gone a long way toward banishing first-night nerves. In this chapter, you will learn how to:

- Keep it short, punchy, and to the point
- Get a laugh without being laughed at
- Organize your material so you and your audience remember it
- Begin with a bang to grab their attention
- Go out on a high note that lasts long after you've left the stage
- Practice for perfection

Keep It Short

There's an old joke about a speaker who begins: "I apologize for giving such a long speech today, but I didn't have time to write a short one." A succinct presentation takes just as much planning as a long one.

Keep It Focused

An organized, concise performance will always be far more effective than a rambling one. The most common fault in presentations is that people try to fit too much in. When it comes to presenting, less is best because:

In presentations, less really is more

- The maximum number of key points an audience can take in and recall later is four or five at most. Any more and you only dilute your point.
- However formal the situation, presentations are an exercise in the spoken word, and speech tends to be much simpler and to the point than the written form. Pick up a business document and read it out loud and you will find that it sounds wordy and stilted. Write a presentation as if it were a document rather than a talk, and it will suffer the same fate.
- Keeping it short means you are unlikely to lose focus, or forget what comes next.

Stay On Message

HIGH IMPACT

- Using straightforward, everyday language
- Keeping your messages short, direct, and punchy
- Keeping your presentation well structured and to the point

NEGATIVE IMPACT

- Using a lot of unexplained technical terms or jargon
- Using clichés and dull, wordy marketing-speak
- Borrowing elaborate phrases from corporate brochures

- No audience ever complained about being released early for a coffee break.

Brevity doesn't just apply to the overall length of a presentation. Short is also sweet when it comes to sentences and individual words. No sentence should ever take more than one breath to complete; you should be able to deliver each one clearly without pausing, or having to organize it in your head. Glance over your notes, looking to see if you have many words of more than two syllables; if you have, ask yourself if there isn't a shorter, punchier way of delivering your message.

Keep It Natural

Don't be afraid to be yourself. People writing presentations often think they will sound more knowledgeable or authoritative if they pepper their speech with lofty language, borrowed buzzwords, or technical terms. This may have the unfortunate effect of making you sound unnatural, verbose, or, even worse, pompous and unapproachable. In reality, the best public speakers generally use the simplest language possible, because it has the most direct effect. When you read your presentation aloud, ask yourself if you would use those terms or phrases when talking to people in an everyday situation. If you don't, change the language.

Using Humor

A touch of humor is a wonderful thing and can lift the tone of a presentation while fixing it in the memory of its audience. But there is a big difference between adding a sprinkling of humor and telling a joke.

Keep to the Point

Even professional comics don't tell a joke cold. They have warm-up routines, or other warm-up acts to help create a mood before they start a patter that eventually leads to the punchline. After-dinner speakers wait for a whole meal full of good cheer to pass before they risk telling jokes to an audience. As a presenter, your job is to focus your audience on your key points, so even if you tell a joke brilliantly and get a laugh, you are only distracting them unless the joke relates directly to the point you are making. Think instead about ways of adding humor that can relate to your point. Cartoons on screen, or

Appropriate Humor Works If you decide to bring humor into your presentation, keep it light, on-message, and easy to appreciate.

CASE study: Borrowing a Punchline

Ray, a public relations executive, had felt that the dry humor he'd been using in his presentations had become rather tired. So he began a presentation with a slide showing a quote from the humorist H. L. Mencken: "The proper relationship of a journalist to a politician is that of a dog to a lamp post." The phrase released a wave of laughter.

• *The humor worked better than Ray's usual dry jokes because he didn't need to read the slide out, but could let its message sink in with his audience.*

• *Having relaxed his audience with easy humor, Ray's presentation got off to a good start and set the scene for some enthusiastic audience interaction.*

appropriate and amusing quotes borrowed from well-known humorists, are far easier to use for your own purposes and much less risky to deliver than jokes. Best of all are anecdotes because, unlike jokes, they can serve more than one purpose. A really great anecdote not only introduces a touch of humor, but helps to illustrate a real-life situation. That way the point still stands even if the humor itself falls flat.

Avoid Forced Humor

A presentation that is humorless but to the point is preferable to one in which the presenter is clearly desperate for the audience to laugh with him. If you know you aren't a natural comic, don't try to force yourself to be one. In situations where humor really is important, such as motivational talks, think instead about ways of letting the props tell jokes for you. A cartoon slide, an amusing picture, or a quote on screen can lighten the tone without requiring any delivery skills.

TIP **Don't risk a tasteless joke. Even if a few people laugh, any success will be far outweighed by those who find the joke offensive.**

Structure Your Presentation

The old truism about presenting is that first you tell them what you're going to tell them. Then you tell them. Then you tell them what you told them. It's a tried-and-trusted technique, but it still takes skill.

Keep It Clear

A well-structured presentation involves much more than simply repeating the same thing three times. It should consist of

- **An opening bang** Before you even start on your introduction, you want to make a powerful first impression to ensure that you have the full attention of your audience.

- **An introduction** Not just who you are and what your subject is, but the reason why the audience would want to pay close attention to you and your arguments.

- **Your key points** If you've taken the advice in the preceding sections, these should be easy to remember and deliver because there are only a handful of them. Every key point you make should be accompanied by a real-world example or anecdote.

5 minute FIX

Your color checklist (see opposite) can serve as a check on a presentation that has been made before.

- Read through, making the appropriate marks as you go.

- If the color pattern doesn't match the ideal template, it's time to reach for the editing pencil.

- **Your closing remarks** If your audience remembers nothing else, they should remember your closing remarks—which is why the end of a presentation usually consists of a summary of key points. Try to do more than that, however, and turn the end into a grand finale by finishing on a high note, with an unforgettable image to help fix it in the audience's minds.

Coding a Presentation

Write out your presentation in rough form, then take colored pencils or highlighters and, using one color for each element, mark out the divisions clearly:

→ the opening "bang"
→ the introduction
→ each key point and its example
→ your summary
→ the high note that fixes it all in their memory

Now that you have all these elements, look at the color pattern you have created. Copy the pattern so a dash of the appropriate color stands for each element, including a separate dash for each key point and one for its associated example. What you have is an instant color-coded checklist and memory jogger. Just by looking at it, you should be able to recall your entire presentation, delivering it as you check off each color in turn.

Your Notes Are Your Script Your notes can remind you of far more than just the words—treat the highlighted points as your stage directions.

Opening Gambits

We've all sat through dull presentations, and audience expectations are likely to be low as you start to speak. This is actually an advantage —it makes it easy to surprise them, and gain a roomful of rapt listeners.

Make the Right Start

The purposes of the opening bang may be several:

- To wake up a tired or drifting audience
- To give them a mental "bookend"—a memorable divide between the last presentation and your own
- To set the scene for a theme or image
- To challenge an assumption
- To create a role or persona for yourself
- To introduce an argument.

Different bangs are therefore needed for different situations. Bursting a balloon with a pin would certainly wake up a dozing crowd and provide a mental bookend,

CASE study: Waking Up the Audience

Sonja, the IT director of a clothing retail chain, knew that she would have to get the audience on her side before engaging them with her subject. She decided on shock tactics. She stood up with a single slide behind her, of a white rhinoceros looking straight at the audience. "This is how most of you see the IT department," she began; "thick-skinned, short-sighted, and charging all the time." She went on to show how much the investment in IT had saved the company that year, by reducing costs and speeding up business processes.

- *Sonja's use of humor had a light touch: the slide provided the joke, while she had only to deliver the punchline. It was also a fine example of challenging the audience's presumptions head on.*
- *As an experienced presenter, Sonja knew that the following presentation must be compelling. She ensured that it was; the risk she overcame was that, if the audience was not engaged, they could leave with that initial image still fresh in their minds. She taught her audience a valuable lesson in effective presenting.*

but unless your presentation is about sudden noises or the sharpness of pins, it won't lead naturally into your introduction. An earth-shattering fact, a powerful statement, or a challenge, on the other hand, could have the same effect as the balloon but also form the beginning of an introduction to your subject.

Use the Unexpected

Shock tactics can get you instant attention. For example, at a meeting of newspaper advertising executives, one presenter stood up and told them that their business was dead and they would all be out of a job in ten months. In fact the presentation focused on the threat the Internet posed to the classified advertising business, and ways in which newspapers could counter it or even profit from it. By opening with a cold-blooded threat to their livelihood, though, the presenter ensured that everyone in the room sat up sharply and paid careful attention to the message.

> **It is best to begin with a bang, not with a whimper**

Begin with a Question

One of the best ways of making an audience pay attention is to start off with a question. Throwing a question out to the audience and taking answers from individuals prompts a response, and gets people thinking. Asking how the audience relates to the subject at hand will encourage them to focus on the issue while picturing themselves as part of it—which makes them much more inclined to listen to you. Just be sure that the answer to your question doesn't derail the rest of your presentation.

> **To begin is half the work. Let half still remain. Again, begin this, and you will have finished.**
>
> Decimus Magnus Ausonius

Begin at the Beginning

Introducing yourself with your name, your job title, and the subject matter of your presentation may cover the basics, but it's like introducing yourself to someone at a party with your name, rank, and serial number.

Give Them a Reason to Listen

If you want to charm someone you've just met, you give them some information about yourself that provokes their curiosity, or even their admiration. The same holds true for a presentation audience. If you want them to listen to what you have to say, you need to give them a reason. Anyone who starts with "I'm here because I am the person who performed the small miracle of balancing the books/ setting up the Azerbaijan office/securing your bonuses for next year" will have the audience's attention. Anyone who opens with "I'm here to talk about finance" will not. "I'm here to talk about finance" doesn't work as an opening gambit because only a handful of people would consider themselves interested in finance.

Take Your Audience with You

See your presentation as a journey. You want the whole audience to travel with you, to follow your logic, and arrive at your point. Set the scene with flair and you will take them with you. Before you set out, however, prepare your audience:

→ Tell them where they are going, why they want to go there, and how much they will enjoy the ride. Make your description compelling, so that they are looking forward to the trip.

→ Rehearse your timing, too, and you'll be able to answer the "are we nearly there yet?" question before you even start.

Speak Their Language

As for introducing the subject matter, the key to success is to introduce the "what's in it for me?" factor

Make Your Presentation a Journey Take your audience with you, and act as their guide, informing and entertaining them along the way.

right away. Announce that you are there to explain new schedules or working practices and eyes will begin to glaze over throughout the room. Explain instead that you are there to make their lives easier, and that 30 minutes of attention now will save hours of frustration and time-wasting next month, and people will want to hear what you have to say. Don't make people work to understand the interest for them—make it clear right from the start.

TIP Think how you would tell your mother what you do and use the same simple explanation—don't introduce yourself with an obscure job title.

Sustain Your Pace

Having made a successful start, keep the pace going through the middle part of your presentation. Remember that every story has a beginning, a middle, and an end, and every presentation should tell a story.

Secure Your Delivery

When you are giving business information, your beginning should always concentrate on the need. Once the need-to-know has been set out, it should be followed by the information itself, and then the solution, or the course of action to follow. You should be clear about what these beginnings, middles, and ends are for each of your key points. Theoretical information is for the classroom, but presentations are for the real world, so wherever possible you should give an example to illustrate each point Concrete details can transform a talk by encouraging the audience to identify personally with the subject matter.

CASE study: Personalizing a Presentation

Janek, a manager for a telecoms company, was staging a session on attitudes to problem solving. He anticipated that his difficulty would be to engage his audience with a discussion on technical problems. His solution was to tell the story of a technical glitch that had caused delays, upset customers, and lost revenue. He described the technical reasons, and explained that one engineer's initiative had solved the problem. The solution, it had turned out, involved an echo tube. The perfect tube turned out to be an empty toilet roll, and the engineer

who found that out was Daryl (at this, Janek pointed to a blushing Daryl, acknowledging the laughter).

• *By giving names and details, Janek turned a potentially dull technical tale into an engaging story, and presented a fellow worker as a role model.*
• *The comic element—that something as basic as an empty toilet roll could solve a complex technical problem—amused his audience and ensured that they remembered his message.*

When practicing your presentation, check each individual statement and point that you are planning to make.
Remember that every statement you make should have its own points of emphasis. Ask yourself what they are at the start and end of each individual statement as you practice.

1 Go through your whole presentation and ask yourself "for example?" every time you make a statement.

2 Can you give a lively and engaging example for each one?

3 Can you make it real?
If there are any points that you cannot bring alive, consider dropping them.

Involve Other People

Your colleagues, family, or friends can be a rich source of examples. If the problem/solutions you're discussing affect them, mention them as part of the key point you are making (this will also help humanize you with your audience—a crowd-pleaser in presentations). If you can offer examples involving members of the audience, that's even better. In addition to examples from people around you, don't be afraid to draw on the strong vein of material on offer from celebrity gossip. Celebrity gossip is in common currency around the world, and whoever your audience is, you can be certain that they will be surprisingly well informed about the lives of the rich and famous. By drawing comparisons with the experiences of the famous, you can establish common ground with your audience and bring a subject to life.

TIP Keep your real-life examples brief—paint the picture in just a line or two—or you may find that they hijack your limelight.

Make a Memorable Finish

The "tell them three times" approach dictates that you end a presentation with a summary of what you just said, a job that can often be done effectively and simply by flashing up the key points in bullet form.

Keep It Memorable

This is certainly better than no conclusion at all, and recognizes the fact that the closing minutes of the presentation are the prime time for recall—what you say then is far more likely to be remembered. You should write your closing remarks on the basis that "if they remember nothing else, they should remember this." There is a potential pitfall, however. Repetition has the effect of dulling a message, so if your closing comments simply repeat your introduction and key message, they may serve only to take the edge off your point. The perfect ending combines a recap with a second "bang" to reinforce it, help memory retention, and provide a "bookend" to definitively draw a line before the next presentation.

Bring Your Argument Full Circle

The grand finale bang differs from the opening one. By this point in your presentation, your audience should be alert and you should already have put your message across, but if your opening bang involved presenting a

Finishing Effectively

HIGH IMPACT	NEGATIVE IMPACT
• Summarizing your argument clearly and succinctly	• Adding a brand new point right at the end of the presentation
• Using a concluding quote or idea that brings the point home	• Saying you missed something, then talking about it
• Firmly thanking the audience	• Apologizing for shortcomings
• Surprising them with a final punchline	• Tailing off, or ending unexpectedly

Points to Conclude with

Your conclusion is the grand finale of the presentation, so it carries a lot of weight. Craft it carefully—it needs to be brief, memorable, and punchy. Make sure that it :

→ Brings matters to a close—if you have to, say "in conclusion," but let people know this is the end.

→ Reiterates the key points—but doesn't add anything new.

→ Opens the way for questioning—presuming that you want a question-and-answer session.

→ Gives people a concise, punchy thought to leave with.

→ Best of all, gives people a course of action to take.

Keep it short—people pay extra attention if you tell them this is the summary, but if you go on too long, they will drift off and miss the most important part of the presentation.

problem or an attitude, you may find that returning to it is a very effective way of finishing off. Ending where you started will also give you a satisfyingly complete feeling. If you've done your job properly, the way your audience felt about the point that you began with will have been colored by the content of your presentation. Finishing with exactly the same bang is a simple way of reminding them of what they thought before you made your presentation. That can be effective shorthand for the point you've made, particularly if it involved overcoming or changing an existing perception.

TIP Conclude with a call to action. Tell people exactly what you want them to do, and suggest they leave the presentation and do it.

Summary: Structuring Well

A well-structured presentation is the first step to getting your message across effectively. Think of your presentation as a story, with a beginning, middle, and end. Follow the steps in this summary and you can look forward to grabbing and retaining your audience's attention, and ending on a high note that lasts long after you have left the stage.

Four Stages to Structure

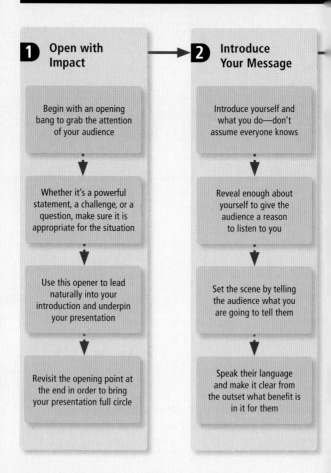

1 Open with Impact

Begin with an opening bang to grab the attention of your audience

▼

Whether it's a powerful statement, a challenge, or a question, make sure it is appropriate for the situation

▼

Use this opener to lead naturally into your introduction and underpin your presentation

▼

Revisit the opening point at the end in order to bring your presentation full circle

2 Introduce Your Message

Introduce yourself and what you do—don't assume everyone knows

▼

Reveal enough about yourself to give the audience a reason to listen to you

▼

Set the scene by telling the audience what you are going to tell them

▼

Speak their language and make it clear from the outset what benefit is in it for them

3 Cover the Key Points

→

4 Summarize and Finish

Organize your core material into key points—four or five at most, otherwise you will lose your audience

Keep each point short, punchy, and focused, using simple language and avoiding clichés

Structure each point so that it has a beginning, a middle, and an end

Reinforce each point with a real-life example or an anecdote—a sprinkling of humor works, tasteless jokes don't

Make it clear that you are at the end of your presentation—the audience needs to know that this is the finale

Summarize the key points— be succinct, and don't introduce anything new

Invite questions (if appropriate), then wrap matters up swiftly

Endpoint
Finish on a high note with a closing impact and a call to action

Watch Your Timing

How long does your presentation take? Have you timed yourself? Having done so, have you allowed for the effect of the audience? You need to know the answers before you begin to ensure a confident delivery.

Rehearse Your Delivery

The obvious way to get an idea of timing is to use a stopwatch while you read through your presentation in practice. That's great to give you a rough idea, but it fails to take into account the factors of the big day. The first is that you may be more nervous in performance than in practice. If large parts of your presentation consist of you speaking, you may tend to speed through them, and finish early. To avoid this, you should practice until your nerves have melted away or consider introducing nonverbal props with which to punctuate points in your presentation, and to take the pressure off you. The other factor to remember is that, if your presentation goes well, then you will need to allow pauses for effect, to let the laughter die down, or to give a transfixed audience time to enjoy the quality of your slides. If there is a lot of audience participation in your presentation, you will either need to work on your crowd control skills or to write more flexibility into your schedule.

When making a point, good timing is everything

5 minute FIX

If you haven't had time to practice, you can still keep an eye on your timing as you give your presentation.

- Mark your presentation at the quarter-, half-, and three-quarter way delivery points. As you reach each point, glance quickly at the clock.

- This helps to avoid clock-watching and alerts you early if your timing is going awry.

Life or Death Timing

A good real-life example of crucial timing comes from the Professional Association of Dive Instructors (PADI). They teach 70 percent of the world's scuba divers to dive.

A diver has very little time to react when things go wrong—and needs to know what to do in the event of a problem, in a literally life-or-death situation. As a result, all PADI instructors present points succinctly. Whether the subject is complex or simple, they are expected to introduce it, explain it, and recap it within eight to ten minutes. In this instance, a dull presentation could have deadly consequences. The mathematics translate well to any subject:

→ Use a maximum of ten minutes per point, with about four key points to a presentation.

→ if you're still talking after 40 minutes, you should be either wrapping up or taking questions.

Time Yourself Check how long each point takes to make ahead of time—you need to be certain you can retain your audience's full attention.

Practice Makes Perfect

While there may be a certain bravado in putting together a presentation on your way to delivering it, unless you really enjoy living dangerously, the key to a successful performance is practice, practice, practice.

Hold Solo and Dress Rehearsals

Truly painless presentations are the result of exhaustive practice. At the very least, you need to have a dry run including any props you intend to use. Ideally you will have run through your presentation so often that you can literally deliver it with your eyes shut, from memory. Having an "unplugged" version of your presentation without slides or aids is not only the surest way of proving you know it by heart, but also makes you bulletproof even if, in the real performance, you encounter technical glitches. Best of all, better even than solo practice, is a full dress

Watch Yourself Even the briefest video clip contains a wealth of information about how you will appear to your audience—watch it carefully.

rehearsal including a pet audience. It helps you get used to having other eyes on you and, if properly prepped, your audience can also throw questions or interjections at you.

Find a Practice Audience

Be wary of relying solely on your friends for feedback—they may not be representative of your audience. One of the best "pet audiences" you can have consists of other presenters who will be able to spot any glitches in your presentation as you rehearse. Find out who else is presenting, and agree to be an audience for each other, even if that just means listening to a quick read-through. This can pay dividends in support on the day, too.

In theory, there is no difference between theory and practice. In practice, there is.

Yogi Berra

The 3
Presenter

It's almost time to begin: the introductions are over, the lights have come up, and, after numerous rehearsals, you're about to step out and make your presentation. If you devote some planning and forethought to your performance ahead of time, you'll find that you are more likely to experience a buzz of excitement than a feeling of fear. This chapter shows you how to:

- Dress appropriately
- Feel comfortable with an audience
- Deal with nerves
- Prepare yourself for predictable problems
- Work the room like a professional
- Use a microphone

Dress to Impress

Knowing you're correctly dressed, and the confidence that that knowledge gives you, is the first step to a successful presentation, and one you can always get right with a little forethought.

Dress Comfortably

Athletes have a time-honored rule that you wear nothing new on race day. The heat of the big day is not the moment to find out that your new outfit chafes, or constricts your movements. For presentations, this is doubly true. You don't need anything that might make you feel self-conscious and, unlike the athletes, visible sweat marks under your arms will certainly not be something to take pride in. Dress to fit in. Women presenters have long known that a few well-chosen accessories can instantly fine-tune the tone, while men tend to presume that a jacket and tie are all they need. Think a little about how your best presenting outfit could be made to fit in if it turns out to be dress-down day. Sometimes taking off your jacket and tie to reveal a stylish vest can send signals about dressing well without being buttoned-down.

TECHNIQUES
to practice

Learn to think carefully about the role you will play in a presentation—and how to dress for it.

Are you the in-house person explaining to colleagues, or an expert from another company?

1 Stand in front of the mirror. Imagine that your role is shown in a caption above you.

2 Are you overdressed? Do you look too informal?

3 Does your image need fine-tuning? Think about how the wardrobe department would dress you if you were playing this role in a movie.

4 If you feel that you need to, adjust your clothes to fit in with your image.

Send an Appropriate Message

Think about your audience when deciding what to wear. There are various ways in which you can try hard, but still send an inappropriate message through your outfit.

Your audience will see how you look before they hear what you say. If you've chosen something very eye-catching or something that makes a specific point, but one that may be lost on your audience, it may actually detract from your message, or reinforce your message in an undesirable way. Some examples are:

→ A presenter in a technical field, showing some new developments, dressed in a Star Trek costume. It was bold, a good joke, and struck a chord with Trek fans in the audience, but to those yet to be convinced about the technology, his presentation seemed even more like science fiction.

→ A financial advisor talking to a skate-wear company wore full boardroom uniform. In a conventional setting, it would have been suitable, but he sent the message to his young, hip audience that financial planning was not for people like them.

→ A woman presenter addressing a largely male conference let her hair down and wore a short skirt. She got the audience's attention, but the way she was dressed detracted from what she had to say, rather than reinforcing it.

Dress Effectively

HIGH IMPACT

- Wearing a neat, simple look to appeal to the audience
- Using color or accessories to stand out from the crowd
- Picking clothes that will underline your image and reinforce your message

NEGATIVE IMPACT

- Wearing clothes that look good but feel uncomfortable
- Choosing overly garish, sexy, or distracting clothes
- Picking clothes that will alienate your audience and undermine your message

Present Yourself with Care

What you wear to present will combine with your body language to create the first impression your audience will have of you. Even a comparatively informal presentation deserves careful dressing: anything less shows a lack of respect for your audience, and for yourself.

Good Grooming
Grooming is a crucial part of self-presentation. Be sure your hair is neat, your clothes are clean and uncreased, and your general "look" is tidy.

Judge Your Audience
You may not need a jacket—or you may take it off—but a dress shirt and, usually, a tie are desirable in all but the most informal settings.

Think about Details
If you aren't wearing a jacket, pants will look more finished with a belt. Similarly, cufflinks, or, for women, a neck scarf, will add polish.

Filmed Presentations

Large presentations are often filmed and projected onto a big screen. If that's the case in the venue in which you are presenting, then you need to follow the dress guidelines that TV presenters use. Expanses of shiny white clothing or "noisy" patterns will dazzle and distract. If you're concerned about the outfit you're proposing to wear from the technical viewpoint, seek out and talk to the video technician the day before you present. Remember, too, that the large scale of the screen means that small details will be magnified, and that this applies to how you wear your clothes as well as everything else. Every politician knows that even a simple touch, like rolling up your sleeves, is a powerful way to change the signals that you send out, transforming you from one of them to one of us.

Check Your Outfit

Ask yourself the following questions when you're assembling your final outfit. If you can confidently answer all the answers positively, you are fully prepared:

→ Am I going to be comfortable in this?
→ If it's hot or cold, and I need to remove or add layers, will that be easy? Will I still look professional when I've added/removed a layer?
→ Do I have spares (and wet wipes) in case of any spills before my presentation?
→ If I suddenly had to look dressier or more casual, could I adjust my clothes to change my image?

TIP Try a costume change—even taking off your jacket can act as a signal that you are now at a new stage of the presentation, such as a Q and A session.

Deal with Nerves

Stage fright always plays a part in presenting. Some professionals claim that a little fear can actually improve a performance. However, there are a number of techniques that you can use to bring it under control.

Establish Why You are Frightened

The first step toward conquering your nerves is to try to identify just what it is that is making you anxious in the first place. Is it just a bit of butterflies in the stomach? That's normal, to be expected, and probably a very good sign (over-confidence is every bit as dangerous as nervousness). If, however, you break into a sweat at the thought of presenting, or have already used every excuse you could think of to get out of presenting, then it's time to face up to your fears, and deal with them one by one.

Rationalize Your Fear

Ask yourself how your fear would be expressed if you were telling a friend.

- "I can't stand up in front of all those people. I'll look like such a fool."
  You won't. But if you don't believe it, think about ways of taking the spotlight off yourself and projecting it onto something you show people, or right back at the members of the audience. Ask yourself if you would be as nervous if it were a round-table discussion. No? Then turn it into one, with yourself as host and guide.

- "My presentation just won't be good enough."
  Turn back to the previous section on content, and make sure you've covered all the points it raises. That done, you can be sure that your presentation will work.

When written in Chinese, the word "crisis" is composed of two characters. One represents danger, and the other represents opportunity.

John F. Kennedy

Maintain Pre-Presentation Confidence

If you are an inexperienced presenter, it is likely you will find that you feel at your most nervous in the final few minutes before you are due to present.

This is the point at which professional presenters move into a well-practiced last-minute routine. You should do the same. Follow these last-minute tips to make sure you are calm and composed before you rise to speak.

The last few minutes are the best time to focus ahead

→ Don't discuss your presentation with anyone. Many people will ask you what you're going to talk to them about by way of pre-presentation small talk.
→ Don't be tempted to get into conversation about it. If they seem unimpressed, they may undermine you; if they offer their own opinions, it may confuse you, or, worse, you may be tempted to rejig your perfectly prepared presentation.
→ Smile politely and tell them that all will be revealed very soon.

Last-Minute Preparation

HIGH IMPACT

- Having a small drink of water, so your throat isn't dry
- Chatting with friendly faces, ideally people you already know, to calm your nerves
- Checking that you have a handkerchief in your pocket, any props you are using are in place, and any notes you need are in order and accessible

NEGATIVE IMPACT

- Drinking too much coffee: a small cup may help, but more will probably increase your nervousness
- Striking up conversation with anyone you don't know: this is not a good time to meet people
- Taking a tranquilizer, an alcoholic drink, or any other unreliable stimulant

Maintain Clarity

Probably everyone's reaction the first time they present is "Why does this have to be me?" This fear usually comes from the idea that other people, some of whom may be in the audience, know more about the subject than you do. The answer is that you are doing the presentation, not writing the book. Unless you are a world expert delivering a new scientific paper, there will always be someone who knows more than you, but that's not the point. Television presenters may know no more about their subject than the content of the teleprompter, but they don't worry about that because their job is to explain someone else's understanding to an audience. Remember that your key strength is clarity rather than depth of knowledge.

Mask Your Nervousness A calm delivery will take your audience with you up to the point at which you feel that all is going well, and can relax.

Eliminate Fear

If you find that in the last few minutes your fears come to a head, remember that some of the greatest actors in the world suffer from stage fright—and find it enhances their performance. Deal with those last-minute gremlins firmly, decisively, and without letting them begin to undermine your confidence.

- "I'm going to freeze or forget." Cheat. Have crib sheets in strategic locations. Ask your friends to ask questions from the audience if the worst happens (and you'll find that if you've prepared, it won't).

- "I just get terrible stage fright." Make it easy on yourself by practicing over and over until you can do the presentation in your sleep.

- "I'll make a mistake." So what? You're human; humans make mistakes. What matters is how you pick yourself up and move on. A stumble may even win the audience over—many of them may be less than confident about presenting themselves, and will sympathize with your nervousness.

- "What if they don't like me?" Does it really matter? It is the message that counts, not the messenger, and if you deliver it strongly enough, the audience will be judging it, not you. If you are concerned about not being a strong presence, compensate with strong content instead.

> **I am a great believer in luck, and I find the harder I work, the more I have of it.**
>
> Thomas Jefferson

5 minute FIX

Fill the final minutes before you present with calming talk with someone who you know.

- Find a colleague who has been in the same position and chat for the last few minutes.

- If you know them well enough, confide your worry to them.

- Even casual chat will calm you; a word or two of reassurance will be even better.

Anticipate Small Problems

The best ad-libs are prepared in advance. Prepare a few all-purpose remarks or jokes to cover up when things go wrong, while you get back on track. The knowledge that you have backup will make you feel much better.

Learn from the Experts

If you stay relaxed, you can use the glitches in a presentation to bond with your audience. Bill Gates, CEO of Microsoft, was presenting to hundreds of developers in San Diego when he was seized by a sneezing fit, right into the microphone. When he finally stopped (remember, always have a handkerchief handy), a joker in the audience shouted "Bless you!" At which he looked up, blinked, and said "Wow, user interaction." It may not have been hilarious, but it was good enough to raise a chuckle, and he bought enough time to find out where he had left off.

Prepare Backup in Advance

Almost any interruption can be dealt with smoothly if you stay calm. One technology speaker ran completely dry at one point and stared blankly at his audience for a few seconds. He had the presence of mind to call out to a

think SMART

Consider what might go wrong in advance of your presentation, and have a plan of action prepared.

Prepare your covering comment—an ironic remark or joke to make light of a problem, while demonstrating that you are not thrown off by it. Make sure you have someone else there to help out with any technical problems so you can continue to talk to your audience while the projector/computer is being set up or restarted. If a technical problem becomes a time-waster, think about where you can send your audience for a two-minute "stretch break" while you sort it out.

friend in the back row, and ask him what came next. His friend, armed in advance with a printout of the presentation, calmly told him his next line. "You see," beamed the presenter, before continuing, "the importance of teamwork." Teamwork was one of the themes of the day, and this particular act was scripted into the presentation, but armed with a similarly themed excuse (teamwork, backup, or fallback plans could all be invoked here), you, too, can ensure that you have a prompter in the wings. The more relaxed you can keep yourself during any hiccups, the better you'll come over to your audience. Another speaker was halfway through discussing the slide on the overhead projector before she noticed it was upside down. She kept her cool admirably: "I'm so sorry," she said as she righted it, "my last speaking engagement was in Australia."

Deal with Unwanted Noise

Passing sirens can be acknowledged and dismissed with a simple one-line joke that brings the focus back onto you. Try, "That's funny—they're not supposed to come for me until after the presentation." To deal with a cell phone ringing in the audience, "Tell them I'm busy" is all you need to say to bring the focus back on yourself.

TIP Ask everyone to make sure their cell phones are switched off before you start, to avoid unnecessary interruptions.

Practice Stagecraft

Actors don't stay in one spot to deliver their lines—they move and gesture to add emphasis. You need to do the same to turn your presentation into a performance.

Weigh Up the Advantages of a Podium

Conventional wisdom among presenters is that you shouldn't use a podium because it hides you from your audience. Worse, it can make you look like a priest preaching from a pulpit, or a judge delivering a verdict. While these factors make podiums a poor option for an informal presentation, there are times and places when these associations could work in your favor. Think about whether the podium might help give you gravitas, or if it will make you look like a severe authority figure. Good podium players step in and out of a role by delivering part of a presentation from the podium and part from the front of the stage, effectively playing a double act.

Think It Through

Think ahead, and run through the following points so that, by the time you come on stage, you know exactly where you will be standing, and how and when you will be moving around:

→ Will there be a podium for you to use if you want one?
→ How tall is it? How will you look behind it? (If in doubt, visit your location the day before and get a friend to take a picture from the back of the room.)
→ If there is a microphone, is it attached to the podium?
→ If you are going to move to and from the podium, have you choreographed your moves?
→ Are the key members of your audience likely to respond well to the perception of authority?

Using a Podium

HIGH IMPACT

- Having somewhere to lay your notes, putting you in a more relaxed frame of mind and helping you to deliver a better presentation
- Moving from podium to center stage and back again, helping to keep the audience's attention focused on you
- Standing relaxed behind the podium, allowing your face and hands to deliver your message

NEGATIVE IMPACT

- Reading notes as if off a lectern, encouraging you to adopt an "eyes down" stance, and stopping you from engaging with the audience
- Moving to and from the podium too many times, making your delivery appear restless and wandering
- Gripping the podium tightly, making it look as though you are using it for support

Use Positive Body Language

You have already considered who you represent to your audience, and your body language should now be all about projecting that identity. Small, informal "one of us" presentations may work better if you're sitting down rather than standing in front of your audience. Consider the dramatic difference between the message sent out by someone sitting behind a desk and someone who comes out from behind it and perches on the front edge of it. The most emphatic way of all to identify with your audience is to sit among them. This may not always be possible, or even appropriate in larger or more formal gatherings, but you might want to consider a move from the front to the middle of a small group at a distinct point in your presentation—it can mark a change in the mood, and work as an effective signal that a brainstorming session or a discussion is about to start.

TIP If you plan to sit or perch on anything, check that it is sturdy enough before the presentation.

Using Body Language

Body language includes everything from your facial expression to the way you stand and move your arms. It makes a huge impression on your audience, so it's worth taking the time to get it right.

Remember to Smile

The first and most important piece of body language is your smile. Smiling shows that you are relaxed and happy to be there; it also helps to warm up the audience. A smile increases your credibility by suggesting confidence and an upbeat attitude. Most people will smile back if you smile at them, and once direct and friendly eye contact has been made with an individual, they are more likely to continue to look straight at you from then on.

TECHNIQUES *to* practice

The mirror makes an excellent practice tool when it comes to rehearsing your body language.

- Stand in front of a full-length mirror and deliver your presentation.
- You'll find that you're consciously making the effort to look yourself in the eye. That's how you want to address your audience.

- Smile at yourself, and practice until your smile looks natural—a forced grin will make you look uncomfortable.
- Practice quickly glancing down at your notes, immediately finding your place, then looking right back up again at your reflection. Remember, you should be spending more time smiling at your reflection than reading your text.

TIP Some body language is offensive in some cultures. Be aware that sweeping gestures or showing your palms may offend in some countries.

Project the Right Attitude

Make sure that the way you stand sends out the right message. Practicing in front of a mirror will help, but remember your stance as you deliver the presentation, too.

Body positions to try:
- → Face your audience with your shoulders relaxed, standing square on to them.
- → Put your hands in your pockets if it makes you feel comfortable—but keep them still once they're there.
- → Keeping your hands loose at your sides may require some effort, but it gives a natural effect.

Body positions to avoid:
- → Hands folded in front of you at groin level.
- → Hands folded behind you: this can look oddly constrained.
- → Arms folded across your chest—this is a protective gesture and can look defensive.

Body Language Speaks Volumes Looking in the mirror may reveal that poses you thought looked casual work well, while others look too rigid or formal.

Work the Room

Unless you're delivering a slideshow in a dark room, people want to see you, so don't hide off to one side: take center stage and be prepared to move around.

Script Your Movement

Moving around the room is an effective way to fix attention on yourself, to emphasize your points, to maintain audience interest, and even, if you hit an awkward hiatus, to buy you time to remember what comes next. Consider the different steps in your presentation and think about how you might break them up for yourself and your audience by delivering them from different spots. Even if you give much of your presentation from one side of a screen, you will focus attention on yourself and your message by taking center stage at the end for your finale.

> **Good presenters match their movements to their delivery**

Walk Tall

If you are going to walk, whether from one side of the stage to the other, or even up a central aisle, be aware that people will be turning in their seats to watch you. Make it worth their while: move confidently, gracefully, smoothly, and slowly with your head held high and your body "open." How you look as you deliver your presentation will affect the audience's perception of what you say. If you walk with your head down and hands behind your back, you may look like an old-fashioned schoolteacher; if you pace restlessly, you will recall a caged animal and make everyone uncomfortable and nervous.

TIP Don't be afraid to move unused whiteboards or other stage furniture to one side before you start your presentation.

The Lighthouse Technique

Even if you can't move around the room, make sure that your eyes do. Don't stare fixedly into space, at your notes, or at your own projected presentation; instead, use the lighthouse technique to "sweep" the room, looking from side to side at the whole audience.

Move Your Gaze Look systematically across the room, "sweeping" the audience with your eyes. If it is feasible, you should try to make eye contact at some point with each and every member of the audience.

Glance at Individuals Let your gaze alight on one person at a time before moving off again. Try not to fix on a single friendly face; if you do, you can end up appearing to address just one person.

Keep Your Eyes Moving This will ensure that you see everything that is going on in the room and remain aware—whether someone wants to ask you a question, or some others aren't paying attention.

Using a Microphone

Once the preserve of the professional speaker, microphones are now making an appearance at even informal occasions. Microphones are easy to use and will help your delivery; you will be given one of three types.

Podium Microphones

The least user-friendly type, because it is fixed to the podium—which tends to mean that you are, too. If you are going to be using a podium mic, your words and hand gestures are going to have to do the work of keeping your audience interested. If confronted with a podium microphone, ask if the venue has another variety available—sometimes you will be offered a choice.

Stand Microphones

The microphone on a stand doesn't obscure your body and can usually be unclipped to become a microphone on a wire, so you can walk around with it (within limits). There are a couple of classic pitfalls. The first is when the stand is not set to the right height and it resists being reset. This results in a presenter either bending down or gazing at the ceiling, neither of which looks impressive. Practice adjusting the microphone stand before you take the stage and stick a small piece of marker tape at the perfect height for you as your rehearse. Leave it on the stand, then, if you are following a taller or shorter speaker, it will be easy for

Microphone Types

TYPE	ADVANTAGES AND DISADVANTAGES
Podium	Gives you a fixed place to deliver from; only your head and shoulders will be seen.
Stand	Can be detached and held in the hand; often awkward to set.
Lapel/Radio	Small and portable; the volume can sometimes "slip."

you to adjust the stand to
the right height. If it's
tricky, arrange in advance
for a helper to come on

A Microphone Is an Aid Don't see it
as a threat: if your voice is quiet, it will
ensure that you are heard.

and do it for you. If you unclip the microphone and start to
walk, be careful not to trip over the cable or let it pull you
up short like a dog on a leash. Remember that holding the
mic means you are left with only one free hand to gesture
with, and tailor your body language accordingly.

Lapel/Radio Microphones

The best sort of microphone by far—unobtrusive, it leaves
you entirely hands-free. It clips onto your clothing and
connects either by wire or by radio to a power pack. Ask
for your mic to be set up and sound-checked before your
turn. Then have it left on, but with the sound turned all the
way down. When it's time for you to talk, the engineer has
only to bring the sound back up to the prearranged level.

TIP Wear a jacket: you can clip the lapel mic on,
and put the power pack in the pocket.

Summary: Stagecraft

It's natural to be daunted by the thought of taking center stage to make a presentation, but some forethought and careful preparation will make the whole process less nerve-racking. Use this summary to help you prepare for your moment in the spotlight—and remember, even the best presenters get nervous beforehand.

Plan of Action

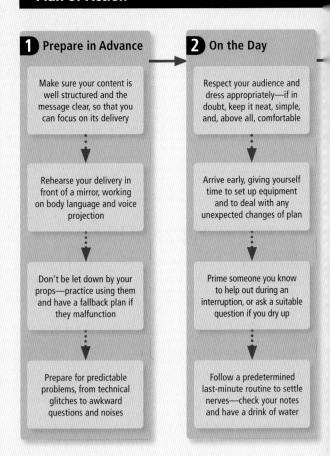

1 Prepare in Advance

Make sure your content is well structured and the message clear, so that you can focus on its delivery

Rehearse your delivery in front of a mirror, working on body language and voice projection

Don't be let down by your props—practice using them and have a fallback plan if they malfunction

Prepare for predictable problems, from technical glitches to awkward questions and noises

2 On the Day

Respect your audience and dress appropriately—if in doubt, keep it neat, simple, and, above all, comfortable

Arrive early, giving yourself time to set up equipment and to deal with any unexpected changes of plan

Prime someone you know to help out during an interruption, or ask a suitable question if you dry up

Follow a predetermined last-minute routine to settle nerves—check your notes and have a drink of water

3 First Impressions

Take center stage with confidence, knowing that you have prepared thoroughly

Expect to be judged by your appearance and what you sound like early on—first impressions count

Be positive in your body language—a smile and friendly eye contact help to engage your audience

Don't be afraid of using a microphone—see it as an aid to ensuring that you are heard

4 Staying Focused

Harness nerves so that they work for you by converting initial stage fright into energy and excitement

Use the lighthouse technique to sweep the room with your eyes

Work the room, building a rapport with the audience—stand tall and be prepared to move around

Exit the stage on time and don't forget to thank your audience

4
The Props

The right props can lend an impressive finish to a presentation, as long as they are there as extras, not to support the whole structure. If you can deliver an "unplugged," aid-free presentation, then you can be confident that nothing can stop you from giving a strong performance. But you can still use props to add sparkle and drive your point home. In this chapter, you will learn how to:

- Use other people as props
- Make the most of whiteboards, flip charts, and overhead projectors
- Create computer presentations that stand out from the crowd
- Add the bells and whistles of sound and animation

Use People as Props

Stage magicians use glamorous assistants whose real function is to distract the audience from the magician's sleight of hand. A business presenter, too, may use people as props to distract, entertain, or inform.

Share Your Spotlight

An assistant can help make your point or divert attention away from you at some points in the presentation, enabling you to be a more relaxed and thus a more compelling speaker. Sharing the stage with colleagues can help you in a number of ways:

- You can borrow their expertise to explain complex or specialized subjects.
- You can work with someone more technically skilled than you on complex computer presentations.
- You can demonstrate that you are a team player, involving your staff in all aspects of your work.
- You can involve someone else to act as the "face" of difficult topics, or a subject on which you know less.

think SMART

The effect of introducing a "guest star" to your presentation will be disproportionate—even if all they are going to do is reinforce your own points.

Like a cameo appearance on a television show, the mere fact that they are there will make your audience sit up and take more notice of your presentation. Your "guest star" can be a more senior member of staff (a little judicious flattery may work well in getting them onto the platform), or an authority from outside the company. Whichever you choose, taking the option of bringing someone who has gravitas in the area in which you are presenting on stage is an effective way of saying that it's not just you who holds this opinion.

CASE study: Using Your Colleagues

Wei worked for a software company and was responsible for marketing brand-new prototypes, but was always extremely anxious lest one of them let him down as he demonstrated. He shared his concern with a colleague, who suggested that he ask one of the company technicians to join him to put the software through its paces. The new form of presentation diminished Wei's nerves and increased his skills as a presenter.

- *Sharing the stage, Wei felt more relaxed; now that he knew that there was no risk that he would have to cope with any technical glitches, his presentations were no longer marred by evident nervousness.*
- *If any problems arose, Wei went on presenting while they were fixed. He was never at the keyboard when a prototype program crashed, so could remain objective as he presented.*

Learn from the Experts

If your presentation involves demonstrating something that may go wrong, it is a good idea to get the person best qualified to do the demonstration onto the stage. If there is a problem, they can fix it, and it needn't spoil the presentation or cause a major hold-up in the proceedings.

Don't Go It Alone

There is strength in numbers, and whether you are simply nervous about being on stage or wary that you are presenting something that will prove unpopular, there is a lot to be said for having a colleague alongside you. If you think that questions are likely to arise to which you won't know the answers, you might consider putting together a panel to help you, and inviting them to share the stage before issuing an invitation for questions or discussion.

TIP **Sharing the limelight can take the nerves out of a performance, but make sure that your co-presenter isn't going to upstage you.**

Using Whiteboards

Whiteboards can be found in offices and meeting rooms around the world because they are cheap, effective, and easy to use. They don't need configuring and you won't have to grope for any hidden switches.

Remember Board Basics

Perhaps it's precisely because you have been so familiar with them from school days onward that the fact that there is a technique to board use is often ignored. The figure of the distracted professor scrawling endless equations on a blackboard is such a stereotype that you presume this is the correct way of using a board. In business presentations, however, the method of delivery is far more important than in academia. Those presenters who try the "absent-minded professor" approach with a business audience forget that it means they end up with their backs to the audience—literally talking to the wall. This is never a good idea. Senior executives may be less disruptive than an audience of schoolchildren would be, but turning your back on your audience for any length of time will make it difficult to keep their attention at all, let alone involve them with what you have to say.

TECHNIQUES *to* practice

Practice your technique in using the whiteboard ahead of your presentation. Your aim should be to use it as a weather presenter would.

- Don't turn your back to the audience, writing as you go. Instead, write your points on the board before you start.
- Cover them with a sheet of paper attached with Blu-tack
- As you present, move the sheet down and reattach it, unveiling the points one by one.
- Face the board only for the time it takes to point at the appropriate detail, or read a single line.

Good Use of a Whiteboard

Keep the time that you spend drawing or writing on the whiteboard to a minimum, and maximize the amount of time spent facing your audience and interacting with them. Give the whiteboard the importance it deserves—as a prop—but don't let it run your presentation for you.

Face the Audience
Aim to continuously point, turn, and talk. Break up what you write into short points, write fast, and turn to read or discuss them as you go.

Prepare Material in Advance If you need any graphics or other time-consuming elements, draw at least an outline on the board in advance.

Use Volunteers If you really need a large amount of text written up, call on someone from the audience to help, so that you can keep talking as they write.

TIP Always carry fresh whiteboard markers in a range of colors. Make sure you can tell them apart from your indelible flip-chart markers.

Using Flip Charts

Like whiteboards, flip charts don't need plugging in and can't suffer compatibility issues with your presentation. They make it easy to prepare your work in advance, ready to unveil.

Prepare in Advance

The key to using flip charts successfully is to prepare them meticulously in advance. Making it up as you go along can work well in spontaneous, free-flowing presentations, but sooner or later you will find yourself flipping frantically backward and forward through your sheets, trying to find that key message you wanted to emphasize again. Avoid this by writing your key messages out on prepared sheets. Keep a roll of adhesive tape to hand, and when you reach the relevant point in your presentation, produce the sheet with a flourish and stick it up clearly to one side, where it won't get lost in any subsequent shuffle. If you are worried that your handwriting is too messy to be legible, enlist a volunteer who can do the writing for you, leaving you free to face your audience, as well as making your flip chart easier to read.

think SMART

If you want to use pictures in your flip chart presentation, but aren't sure enough of your drawing skills to be happy about drawing in front of an audience, you can prepare your images in advance.

Very lightly pencil or trace the drawing you want to use onto your flip chart. Then, when you need the drawing in the course of your presentation, you have only to run quickly over the lines with a quick marker for your drawing to appear. The guidelines will be invisible to your audience, who will be impressed by your impromptu drawing skills.

Use Good Flip Chart Technique

Just as with whiteboards, there are a few rules to follow that will make your flip chart much easier to use and help to ensure that your audience can always see and read the material you have prepared.

→ If possible, take your own charts to a presentation. When choosing a flip chart, look for types that tear off easily so you can change the order of your presentation if you decide to.

→ Leave a blank page in between charts with a lot of ink—or the following page will show through to the one before.

→ Consider charts that have a grid marked on them—it makes it much easier to maintain a constant letter/word size and helps to keep your writing visible.

→ If you want to change something on a chart, you don't have to throw it away and start again—white-out markers will cover the unwanted words quickly and effectively.

Making Charts Work

HIGH IMPACT

- Using only a few, strong colors
- Writing in large, easy-to-read capital letters
- Leaving an area of clear white space at the bottom of each chart
- Writing key points on sticky labels ready to add to your chart, and using large gold star stickers to mark positive points
- Brainstorming with both a whiteboard and a flip chart: the first for getting the ideas down, the second for listing key points

NEGATIVE IMPACT

- Using old, fading markers
- Writing in hard-to-read lower case or cursive writing
- Using the whole page, so the bottom is hard to see from the back
- Failing to prepare sheets you know you will need in advance, so that you spend much of your presentation writing
- Using just a flip chart in a brainstorming session: you will soon run out of space and it's easy to lose your place

Using Projectors and Slides

The popularity of the PowerPoint presentation has almost eclipsed overhead projectors (OHPs) and slides as presentation tools, but there are still some occasions when you need to use them, so you should know how.

Create the Right Conditions

If you are using slides, the room must be darkened, with the downside that a tired audience may be tempted to doze. Avoid this by ensuring that the room is well ventilated and not too hot. The dark also means that the presenter isn't seen, which—although it may seem a boon if you are self-conscious—means that the impact of the presentation must be made solely with your images and your words. Make sure that you have scripted them carefully, and if you are relying on notes, ensure that there is some local light, so you can read them in your darkened room. Many bookstores sell small clip-on lights for

TECHNIQUES *to* practice

If you are not familiar with projector and slide use, practice carefully in advance to be sure your presentation has a professional edge. Work through the following points:

1 Rehearse your speech and slide order—just because you can't be seen doesn't mean that it's acceptable to read your presentation.

2 Don't be tempted to overdo it and flash up new slides every two seconds; rely on a few powerful images rather than a blizzard of images.

3 If you are only using a few slides, switch off the projector or cover the lens between slides, so that the audience is not dazzled by a blank screen.

4 Remember to turn off the projector (and raise the lights) if your presentation is going to end with a talk, so you aren't trying to compete with the noise it makes.

TIP When each slide has several points on it, only reveal the text as you reach it—or the audience will read ahead and get to the points before you do.

attaching to books for night reading; a clipboard equipped with one of these makes reading in the dark easy without being too much of a distraction.

Stay in Sequence

Overhead projectors can be set up so that you stand behind or among your audience, and they may not always require a darkened room, which makes them an easier option for smaller presentations involving discussion. In most practical ways an OHP presentation is like one using a flip chart, but because slides are readied and presented one at a time, it is easier both to change the sequence and to get it out of order. If your acetates have backing sheets, take them off before you present and keep them in order in a folder. You can also have notes stuck to the side of each one to remind you of the key points to bring up. Another option to try is to make each new point on a fresh acetate and lay it on top of the previous one, to emphasize that you are building up a picture or an argument.

Keep Your Presentations Fresh

When showing slides with bullet points, don't reveal the whole acetate at once

Cover up the points lower down the list with an opaque page; only the heading should show at first

Slide the cover page down to expose each new point as you get to it

Ask your audience to guess what the next point will be before you reveal it. Focus their attention and build anticipation

Using Pointers and Props

A physical prop can be anything that helps reinforce your point or add humor. If you are presenting a product, it makes sense to bring it on stage with you and show the audience what you are talking about.

Make Your Props Effective

Used to your advantage, a physical prop can help fix a point or take the focus off you as presenter. The risk it poses is that it can be distracting unless you ensure that you can make its relevance clear quickly and easily to your audience. Elaborate props that require a lot of explanation defeat their purpose—to divert and entertain the audience—and you run the risk of appearing as the assistant to your prop rather than the other way around. If you are doubtful about the advantages of a prop, get a colleague to watch you while you give it a practice demonstration.

CASE study: Offering Visual Proof

Julio, a fund-raiser, presented regularly on the theme of affordable technology for the third world. He realized that the repetition of his worthy arguments for the desirability or even the possibility of cheap computers was wearing thin on audiences who were tired of hearing appeals for money—he needed a prop to show them. At his next presentation, he put a bright yellow laptop on the table and announced that it could be marketed for under $100. Although what he was showing them was only a model, the technical team had put together, the bright yellow machine caught the audience's attention.

• *The only question Julio needed to ask was "Who wants to be the only one NOT to invest?" He learned that even a purely visual prop can get great results.*
• *For the audience, the sight of the prototype made Julio's presentation seem real; instead of a theoretical goal, he was showing them a reality, and they were energized into wanting to help him make it happen.*

Pointer Skills

At one time it seemed that every presenter had a telescopic pointer that would be tapped noisily at

Lasers Are Unobtrusive Small, discreet, and easy to use, they will ensure the audience's attention stays where it should—on your presentation.

the whiteboard, flip chart, or screen throughout the presentation. A good presentation shouldn't need a pointer to emphasize it. Build your argument with bullet points and transitions rather than tapping your way through it. Much the same applies to any other physical prop. Show it to the audience, but resist the temptation to play with it when you should be talking about it. When it has done its job, place it offstage where it won't distract from any subsequent points.

TIP If you really need a pointer, buy or borrow a laser pointer that fits discreetly in the hand and casts a bright red dot onto your image.

Using PowerPoint

Computer software has taken over the presenting world, and with good reason. The most commonly found program is PowerPoint, which offers a powerful arsenal of features to add impact to presentations.

Get the Balance Right

The downside is that PowerPoint makes it all too easy to overdo it. Computer visuals should be there to help the presenter make their point, not to take over the whole presentation. Even if you are using PowerPoint, you should still be the focus of your presentation—doing the talking and delivering the information. If you fall into the trap of putting the essence of your presentation on screen, you might as well print the whole thing off, hand it out, and go home.

Software should simplify presentations, not complicate them

Sort It Out

One useful feature of PowerPoint (and this also features in most other software packages) is the Slide Sorter view, in the View menu. It lets you see all your slides at once and get an overview of your presentation, and is good for checking that your presentation has a logical progression from start to finish. Because it features all your slides in miniature, you can see if you are cramming information in, and spoiling the overall effect. If you can read the text on your slides when you are looking at them in a reduced size, they are filled with about the right amount of material. If you can't, take a good look at them to see if your font is too small, or if too many words are fighting for space.

TIP Use transition effects but keep them simple. A "wipe" from one side of the screen to the other is effective for replacing screens, for example.

Using Presentation Software Well

Anyone who attends presentations regularly will be familiar with overly elaborate PowerPoint creations, featuring long sequences of slides with too many flashy effects. Here's how to make the best of your software:

→ Break it up—the fewer slides, the better, but not if it means cramming ideas onto them. Five slides with one point on each of them will be much easier to take in than one slide with five points.

→ Signal what's coming next. Use separate slides as "chapter headings" to break up your points and present the information in bite-sized pieces.

→ Boil it down. Slides should consist largely of bullet points that summarize the arguments that you are presenting verbally.

→ Above all, stick to the basic rule: anything longer than a single line of text should be said, not read.

Get a Colleague's View A huge advantage of the PowerPoint format is that it is easy to run through on screen, so it's easy for you to solicit another opinion.

think
SMART

Even though your slides probably feature words rather than images, you will use them better if you think of them as the "pictures" in your presentation.

An analogy might be a storybook for children—the words are there for you to read, while the pictures support them. In the same way, your slides support your words, as the "pictures" in your presentation, but remember that it is your script that is the presentation's main event; your slides should support them, not distract from them.

Make Your Text Work

Remember that the skill of presentation is storytelling and that people want to hear your words, not to look at them. Any words on screen should fulfill one of the following purposes:

- A summary or recap
- A prompt or memory aid for the presenter
- A key fact or figure to hammer home, or provoke discussion
- A quote, when you want to make it clear that you are using somebody else's words.

Words should be spoken, not looked at

One of the surest ways of ruining any presentation is to flash up text on screen, then stand to one side and read it aloud. Don't ever do it: it manages to be pointless, dull, and insulting to your audience's intelligence all at the same time.

TIP Use the spellchecker. Nothing makes a bad impression faster than a misspelled word projected across a large screen.

Keep Your Message Short

The fewer words in a presentation, the better, but be aware that the fewer words there are, the more weight each one will carry. Rhetorical effects, such as the power of three (for example, "I came, I saw, I conquered" or "blood, sweat, and tears") are especially appropriate for presentations. Three slides simply titled "The Good," "The Bad," and "The Ugly'" will be more memorable than a whole series debating the good and bad parts of a review. Don't forget the importance of good grammar and spelling, or that presentation packages have built-in grammar and spellcheckers. If you want to double-check, enlist a friend to read through your presentation. Sometimes you have stared at your slides so often that you no longer really see the words clearly, and it helps to have someone else reassure you that all is well.

Display Your Text Well

Choose your font and text color with care. Since the words are, for presentation purposes, working as pictures, the font you choose is more important than it would be for a document. A gothic font in black or a classic like Times Roman can look authoritative, for example, while Comic Sans in a bright color will be approachable and lively.

→ Stick to that font. Mixing and matching fonts is visually confusing and can end up in a mess of different letters— known as the "ransom note" style.

→ Bullet points are punchy, but they aren't the only way. For maximum impact, consider giving each point its own slide.

→ Anything that looks cramped will be confusing, so leave a double space between lines, and try to keep your words in the middle of the screen, not filling it from top to bottom.

Make Pictures Work

As the preceding pages show, even words can work as pictures in a good

Use Strong Graphics Easy-to-use software produces professional-looking graphics to support any statistics or other figures that you need to feature.

presentation, so it makes sense to use graphics, too, to help boost your presentation's visual appeal. You have a wide variety of options—charts or graphs, clip art, pictures or backgrounds—to enliven your delivery.

Explore Your Software's Possibilities

Presentation software, spreadsheets, and even word processors all have graph-making tools these days, so before showing a slide full of numbers, experiment to see if a graphic approach can make your figures dance on screen. The trick is to rate clarity above all else. The axes on bar charts should make it instantly clear what the bars mean, and any information floating around the sides should be cut. Keep the words surrounding the "pie" to a minimum on pie charts. The best way to do this is to put figures such as percentages into the pie slices themselves.

Find Original Clip Art

A certain amount of clip art probably came included with your presentation software. For basics like bullet points, bombs (for impact), and balloons (for speech) this will work well, but for more noticeable images such as cartoons, it pays to look farther afield, or you risk using the same examples as the presenters before and after you. Type "clip art" into a search engine such as Google and you will find a vast amount to choose from online. Don't mix and match styles, or your presentation will look messy, and don't overload it with images or cartoons, or you will get a comic-book effect. Do check that it is clearly indicated that the images you propose to use are copyright-free, too.

Create Your Own Backgrounds

Pictures are easily added using the Insert menu. Carry a simple digital camera with you and you can capture images of relevant places and even of the audience themselves right up to the last minute, to tailor your talk. Backgrounds are best kept simple so they don't distract, but that doesn't mean they have to be black and white. Key things to look out for are consistency across the presentation, and legibility. A color gradient fill may look good, for example, but it is useless if it makes the last line of text melt into the background. Using knocked-back or faded pictures as backgrounds can be effective and add atmosphere to your screens, but be careful that you don't waste your precious words by making them illegible. To create a knocked-back background, select "Picture" from the Insert menu, choose your image, and insert it into your slide. Then select Washout (sometimes called "Watermark") from the Color icon, and you can convert the image to a subtle, faded version of itself, perfect for laying text over.

TIP **When you have added all the effects you want, go over your presentation as a whole. If it seems overcrowded, edit it down to make it simpler.**

Summary: Using PowerPoint

Computer visuals can add sparkle to a presentation, but it's all too easy to let them take over. Make sure that PowerPoint is helping you to make your point, not acting as the main thrust of your presentation. Use this summary to get the best from your software, giving your presentation a professional look, but without overdoing it.

Making PowerPoint Effective

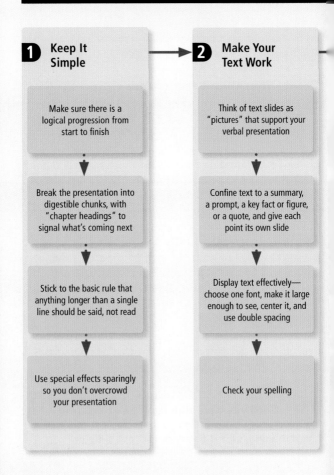

1 Keep It Simple

Make sure there is a logical progression from start to finish

↓

Break the presentation into digestible chunks, with "chapter headings" to signal what's coming next

↓

Stick to the basic rule that anything longer than a single line should be said, not read

↓

Use special effects sparingly so you don't overcrowd your presentation

2 Make Your Text Work

Think of text slides as "pictures" that support your verbal presentation

↓

Confine text to a summary, a prompt, a key fact or figure, or a quote, and give each point its own slide

↓

Display text effectively—choose one font, make it large enough to see, center it, and use double spacing

↓

Check your spelling

3 Add Effects for Impact → **4** Personalize Your Presentation

Use graphics to bring figures and statistics to life—opt for clarity above all else

Boost your presentation's visual appeal with clip art and pictures, but avoid a comic-book effect

Try using faded-out pictures relevant to your audience as effective backgrounds to your text

Add instantly recognizable sounds to reinforce a message or act as a transition between slides

Make your first page a cover page featuring the subject, venue, date, and any relevant logo

Match your examples to the trade or profession of your audience

Incorporate pictures of people in the audience, perhaps as "hidden" slides for when you need a change of pace

Insert a relevant video clip, such as a to-the-point message from a "guest speaker"

Sounds and Animations

Inserting sounds and video is as easy as inserting clip art. Now that even cell phones can make video clips, it is surprising that more presentations don't feature sound and motion—they can make a lively contribution.

Add Sound

To add sound to your PowerPoint slides, go to the Insert menu, select "Movies and Sounds," and pick an effect from your files. Add it to a slide (the software will give you the choice between it playing automatically, or only when you click on it during your presentation). Carefully picked, it's surprising how instantly recognizable many sounds are. Noises like Homer Simpson's "Doh!" or quiz show buzzers (melodious for a right answer, clunking for a wrong one) are a very quick way to make a point. They can also be attached to transitions so that the next slide is "announced" by a sound effect to complete the transition. If sounds are an important factor in your presentation, check the volume and sound quality before you start.

CASE study: Using Classic Effects

Dolores was in charge of a pilot program for a bulk mail sales technique, and the results of the trial research were spectacularly successful. She wanted a quick way to wake her colleagues up and get their interest, but they were used to dancing text and other PowerPoint tricks. Instead, Dolores copied the classic movie trick in which newspaper headlines are shown swirling around and around, before "hitting the desk" with a slap. To recreate the effect, all that was needed was an animated text "headline" with the sound of a heavy newspaper being dropped on the desk attached to it.

• *The effect caused a buzz of amusement as her audience recognized the classic reference.*
• *Dolores learned that it's worth looking beyond the effects supplied for an appropriate way to get your message across.*

TIP If you're using music or video, make sure it is out of copyright. The unauthorized use of copyright material can create serious problems.

Add Video

In addition to sound, video clips can add all sorts of dimensions to your presentation. Video may be a simple way to introduce "guest speakers" into your production: many busy people in senior positions who would be too busy to contribute to your talk in person will be happy to roll up their sleeves and give you a few minutes of their time to make a short video—especially if you think ahead and make it at their convenience, rather than at your own. Think of the video awards speeches given by winners who couldn't make it to the ceremony. Videos are also an effective method to showcase products or services. If any brand-new developments feature in your presentation, a short video in the style of a documentary or news item can be a good medium in which to introduce them. Animating text is also easy in PowerPoint. Click on Slide Show, then Custom Animation, and Add Effect. You can select an effect and apply it to your words if you want them to have extra impact on screen.

Enlist Customers to Your Cause

There's nothing more convincing than a video or audio of the customer delivering a testimonial

Use your camera—or even your phone—to take a simple "talking head" video of a customer expressing their satisfaction

Include the clip in a slide, add a caption, and let the results speak for themselves

Your audience will respond well to "one of them" offering their positive views

Use Professional Tips

The omnipresence of PowerPoint presentations means that if you rely on one, you run the risk of being just another in a long line. Here are some tricks the professionals use to catch and keep attention.

Personalize Your Presentation

There are many ways of doing this, but one of the best in any situation and with any audience is to make it clear that this presentation has been put together specifically for them. The reverse is also true—if your audience begins to feel that you are going through the motions with a stock presentation, they will turn off. So even if you are using a stock presentation, you need to tailor it carefully.

Transport Your Presentation

USB memory keys are cheap and small enough to fit on your key ring, but they can store large presentations along with the PowerPoint viewer software. You can take an instant presentation with you wherever you go. This offers multiple advantages:

→ You don't need to worry about bringing your own machine; you can simply plug your memory key into one already in situ.

→ Memory keys are both Mac and PC-friendly, so you don't have to worry about compatibility.

→ Conjuring up a memory key from your pocket is more elegant (and much less heavy) than transporting your computer.

→ A memory key also serves to back up your presentation, so that if anything goes wrong with the original, you have a spare. Ensure that the one you carry is the latest version.

With technology becoming smaller and lighter all the time, it may be that the USB key is the presentation tool of the future.

TECHNIQUES
to practice

If you present often, use a variety of simple ways to effectively personalize your presentation, and to make it fresh each time:

1 Make your first slide a "cover" page featuring the subject, the date, and the names or the company name of the people present.

2 Acquire or scan a copy of the company logo in advance and insert it into slides or use it as a transparent background. Don't use very low-resolution images, which will pixelate and be unreadable when projected on screen.

3 Scanning and incorporating recent newspaper or trade journal coverage of the company is a simple way to show that you're up to date with events.

4 Include pictures of the people in the audience. If you work with them regularly, this is easy, but even if you don't, you could use a small camera or phone to snap key people before the presentation, and incorporate their pictures.

Gain Extra Time

Hidden slides enable you to build in some protection in case you need to buy more time. They are slides that you can keep in reserve—they don't show up unless you press the button. Prepare your secret slide in advance, then go to the Slide Show menu and click on Hide Slide. The slide shows up in your slide order but won't display to the audience unless you want it to. To use it, arrange your hidden slide to come after the one at which you think you may need the extra material. When you get to the slide before it, just press the "h" key to reveal the hidden slide.

TIP Pressing the "b" key during a presentation will black out the screen (press again to return). Use it to momentarily switch off when digressing.

The 5
Audience

Inexperienced or nervous presenters may find it difficult to rise above their personal fear of presenting. Completely focused on delivering their presentation, they don't consider the audience. Tailoring the presentation to your audience, though, will make it more useful, ensure a better reception, and even turn the audience into an aid to your performance. In this chapter, you will learn how to:

- Read the mood of an audience and give them what they want
- Interact with the crowd
- Tackle questions with confidence
- Handle hecklers
- Assess the reaction, and make a smooth, professional getaway

Read the Mood

If you've done your homework on the "Who?," "What?," and "Why?" issues, then you will already have a good idea of who is in your audience and why they are there. Now you need to know their mood.

Prepare in Advance

Try to gauge the expectations of your audience ahead of your presentation. If you can get a list of attendees with contact details—if you are presenting at a large meeting or a conference, the organizer should be able to supply you with this—send them an email asking what they hope to get out of the presentation. If you get some useful responses, it will help you to tailor your content and delivery to their expectations, but even if you don't, your mail will show that you are going the extra step in tailoring your presentation to them, and that alone may make your audience more receptive.

Empathize with an audience and you have its attention

Present to Individuals

With a small or informal presentation, you may be able to single out key individuals beforehand and ask how they feel about the topics you will discuss. A little flattery about appreciating their input will help. This helps you tailor your topics but also ensures that key people, noting their input in your presentation, are likely to be more warmly disposed to it and to you. Just before you go on, have a chat with audience members. You'll get an idea about how eager, bored, or even resentful they are, and it means you can drop their name into your presentation. For example "I'm sure some of you, like Mira here, are more worried about X than Y." This helps get away from the impression that you're just dumping information and ideas on them, and shows you have considered their point of view. At the very least, Mira is now awake and listening hard.

TIP If the audience seems disengaged, ask them why. Singling out an individual for their input will wake everyone else up.

Assess as You Go

During the presentation, don't stop looking around and reading the audience mood. Transitions aren't just a PowerPoint technique—they also give you a moment to take a break and assess if you are going too fast or slow. For example, you might say, "That's all on the subject of change management; is everyone happy with that before I move on to procedures?" As well as increasing the level of interaction, this helps your audience to divide up a larger presentation and to focus on the next section.

think
SMART

Take the guesswork out of reading the mood by asking your audience to tell you—and in the process have them focus on what they want and what they are getting out of the presentation.

- Asking everyone why they are there works as a great warm-up exercise. It helps people think about what they want to learn.
- Your audience will be surprised when you connect with them in such a direct way—and that means you have their attention.
- Sharing aloud may give others a new idea of the value of what you are showing.

Even if (as may be the case) the answer is that your audience is here because they were told to be, asking the question will help divert any possible resentment they feel about it away from you.

Present in Your Role

In the "Who" section, you asked yourself who you are in the eyes of this audience. You might be the leader, the authority, the entertainer, or the "one of us" figure. Now it's time to get into your role.

Identify Yourself

One of the key factors in who you are going to be is whether or not your audience knows you. It may be reassuring to present to familiar faces, but it also means that your character is already established. If you are seen as the office junior, it may be difficult to demand respect and deliver an authoritative presentation. On the other hand, it could be your chance to create a new image. To make the best of the opportunity, ask a few questions:

- How do people here see me as an individual?
- How do they rate my authority?
- How do they rate my level of knowledge?

Bring On an Expert If you feel that a more experienced voice will support certain points in your presentation, bring on a guest speaker.

Give Yourself Authority

If you want to command the audience, but are concerned about your perceived authority, borrow some from elsewhere.

→ Involve "guest stars," even if only in the form of quotes from more senior staff.

→ Back up your assertions or points with precise references to specialists or events, to make it clear that you have done your research thoroughly.

If, on the other hand, you realize that you may be seen as intimidatingly senior, bring in some more light-hearted elements.

→ Don't be tempted to tell jokes—instead, try opening with a reference taken from a less serious source.

→ Starting with a relevant item from today's newspaper or a reference to a piece of celebrity gossip is an effective way to lighten the tone.

And finally, you should consider carefully how these points will affect your impact on your audience. If you're known as an affable, "one of us" figure, this may work in your favor when you are presenting new procedures or edicts from above. On the other hand, it may undercut you if you are presenting your own initiatives.

Use Humor Wisely

Relaxing though it is to hear an audience laugh, remember that it is your message, not your appeal, that should come first. Instead of telling jokes, use anecdotes or slides to show amusing things other people have done, and you will be focusing the laughter away from yourself.

> **We communicate with passion, and passion persuades.**
>
> Anita Roddick

Interact with Your Audience

If you have ever been to a stage show in which audience members are brought on stage, you will have noticed that the atmosphere changes instantly as people realize they may be required to become active participants.

Introduce the Unexpected

Handled properly, a little audience interaction can:

- Shift the spotlight away from you
- Ensure 100 percent attention from the audience
- Show that you have tailored your topics to your attendees

Bringing audience members to the front of the stage has two effects. It means you're no longer alone out there, and it keeps everyone else on their toes when they see they may be next up. Well handled, it can also be great fun. Consider the following ways of making the audience part of the presentation:

- Ask for a volunteer—whether to write on the board, or be a guinea pig for some other part of your performance; this gives you support on stage.
- Select random guinea pigs—this will wake everyone up as they wonder if they're going to be called on next.
- Read out the names of individuals present and bring them on stage to answer questions, explain a point of view, or take part in an impromptu game.
- Tape envelopes underneath some seats and call up the people seated in them, to perform a task or to help you, depending on the contents of the envelope.

5 minute FIX

Keep control during any games or role play that you introduce to your presentation by:

- Taking a minute or two to explain what's going to happen before you bring people on stage.

- Taking another minute to regroup and calm things down during the game or role-play session if it proves necessary.

TIP **The first presentation after lunch poses the biggest risk of a dozing audience. Begin with a bang and make it clear there will be interaction.**

Involve the Whole Audience

Nicholas Negroponte, professor of Media Technology at MIT, lectures extensively on communications. One of his interactions is to tell the whole audience to start clapping at once and see how long it takes for them all to clap in perfect time (which happens surprisingly quickly, often in less than a minute). In doing so, he has taken a minor party trick and used it to emphasize a point about our ability to harmonize and organize even with complete strangers. He has also succeeded in involving the whole audience without putting any individual on the spot. It requires no props, no preparation, and works with any group of people, from any country or culture.

CASE study: Involving Volunteers

Jules, an academic, gave serious scientific demonstrations. They were greeted in respectful silence, but he felt that involvement was missing. He decided that audience participation was the answer. At his next presentation, instead of performing solo, he asked a member of the audience to hold a sausage, over which he poured liquid nitrogen. The sausage froze, and as the audience was registering this, he poured liquid nitrogen over one of his own hands. A sharp intake of breath was followed by a laugh of relief as the audience realized his hand hadn't frozen. His "experiment" was enthusiastically discussed at the post-presentation coffee session.

• *Jules learned that some humor and irreverence can work better with an audience than any number of dry facts.*
• *The fact that the experiment used one of their number as a guinea pig showed the audience that even serious science can amuse and involve.*

Use Handouts

Handouts are effective backups for presentations, may be used to encourage note-taking, and can prompt attendees to remember you and your presentation long after the chairs have been cleared away. Remember to put contact information on the handouts, both for yourself and (where appropriate) any companies or individuals mentioned in the presentation. Also, if you expect people to take notes, print only on the top half of the page, leaving room so that they don't have to write in the margins.

Handouts should support a presentation, not repeat it

Hold the Audience's Attention

Remember your school days, when teachers told you to open a book to a certain page, and then talked while you read? Don't let that happen in your presentation. Even if you want handouts to cover most of the subject, be sure there are points during your presentation at which you ask your audience to put them to one side and focus on you, not the paper in their hands. If possible, hand out your papers partway through, rather than at the beginning, to ensure the audience doesn't read ahead of you.

Keep Your Options Open

Consider printing up a full PowerPoint presentation and having it ready. Having taken a reading of your audience's mood, you will have the option either of using your PowerPoint slides, or of announcing that you're not going to show them because you'd rather talk informally. Anything that you don't cover in the talk will be contained in the full presentation, which you can hand out to anyone who wants it as they leave.

TIP Most software packages can print multiple slides neatly onto a single page.

Distributing Handouts

Take a moment to think about how and when to distribute your handouts. You might want everyone to start out with a sheet in front of them, or to give them out at the end.

Perhaps your sheets can take the role of a break or transition, so that you pause between subjects to hand out the papers. You can even make handouts part of audience interaction by tailoring certain handouts for certain groups in the audience and inviting the participants to find the appropriate handout for themselves.

→ Don't give out a printout of your slides at the beginning of a presentation: your audience will only skip ahead to your carefully planned points before you want to bring them up.

→ Do consider that an outline plan of your presentation—only the slide titles, for example—may encourage the audience to take notes, which can help them to retain information. You can follow this up by giving a full handout of the slides later.

→ If you take the second option, don't tell your audience in advance; it will discourage them from taking notes.

Keep Audience Attention on You Even if your audience is taking notes and glancing at your handout, ensure that you are the main focus of their attention.

Take Questions

The time will come when your audience wants answers, whether it arrives in the form of casually called-out questions or a formal Q-and-A session. Here are some tips to help you to respond well to questioners.

Think Ahead

Anticipate likely questions in advance and prepare your answers. Even better, if you know there is an area you are weak in, but in which you have a colleague who is strong, then throw the question over to them—though it's best to forewarn them that you're going to do this. Consider including them as a "guest star" in your presentation.

If the question and its answer are dragging on, or it's a difficult subject that you don't want to be drawn on, say that it deserves more time than you can give it in this Q-and-A session and firmly insist it be "taken offline" and dealt with afterward.

Give Honest Answers

Similarly, if you don't know the answer to a question, don't bluff or stall. Instead, make it clear that you don't know, but that you will find out, and promise to get the questioner the answer. If you promise to answer later, deliver on your promise. Take the initiative, seek out the difficult questioner, get their business card or contact details, and set a

The ABC of Taking Questions

Acknowledge
the question:
"Good question" or
"I share your worries about..."

Bridge
back to your own point: "It's because I share your worries that I'm going to talk about..."

Communicate
Get straight back to your own comfort zone of information and opinion, and continue presenting.

If questioners interrupt, ask them to let you finish, in case you answer their question.

time period for your follow-up. Now use that respite to find the answer. Even if you eventually have to admit you can't find an answer, you will still come across as serious and professional—and you won't have to make that admission in front of the rest of the audience.

Be Fearless

Don't be afraid of question time. Nobody likes being caught off guard, but that's often because they fear being isolated in the spotlight. Careful preparation will ensure that you are as ready as you can be for questions, and inviting others to share the limelight, or throwing the issue open to the audience, allows you to turn questions into an informal debate that you can control, rather than making you a target for questioners.

TIP "Good question" buys time while you think, but adding detail, "...the issue of share value concerns us all," sounds much more informed.

Summary: Audience Interaction

If you are a nervous or inexperienced speaker, it's very easy to become so inwardly focused and preoccupied with the ordeal of getting through your presentation that you forget about your audience—yet your audience is your reason for being there. Use this summary to help you to break down the barrier between "me" and "them" and interact with the audience in a lively and positive way.

Routes to Interaction

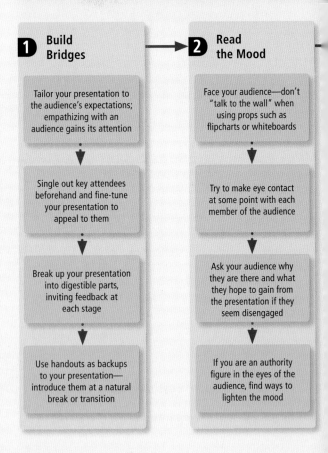

1 Build Bridges

Tailor your presentation to the audience's expectations; empathizing with an audience gains its attention

Single out key attendees beforehand and fine-tune your presentation to appeal to them

Break up your presentation into digestible parts, inviting feedback at each stage

Use handouts as backups to your presentation—introduce them at a natural break or transition

2 Read the Mood

Face your audience—don't "talk to the wall" when using props such as flipcharts or whiteboards

Try to make eye contact at some point with each member of the audience

Ask your audience why they are there and what they hope to gain from the presentation if they seem disengaged

If you are an authority figure in the eyes of the audience, find ways to lighten the mood

 3 Shift the Spotlight

Involve the whole audience—knowing they might have to participate will keep them alert

↓

Stay connected with the audience by using a volunteer to do the writing if you are using a whiteboard

↓

 Use people as guinea pigs to demonstrate a point—or bring on an "expert" from the audience

↓

 Introduce a party trick that involves the whole audience—it can work wonders with a flagging audience

 4 Questions and Answers

Listen to the question, acknowledge it, and restate it for the benefit of the audience

↓

Show that you have done your homework by being able to answer the most predictable questions

↓

 Be honest when you can't answer the question—pass it to an informed colleague, involve the audience, or take it "offline"

↓

 After the presentation, make the effort to follow up difficult questions and get audience feedback

Handle Hecklers

Comedians handle hecklers with ridicule: not an option for a professional presentation. Politicians, though, have to acknowledge the heckler and handle them so they don't distract from the point being made. Here's how.

Find Out Who's Heckling

Not all hecklers are the same. If someone starts to interject as you're presenting, try to identify if they are just attempting to draw attention to themselves or their opinion. There are two main types of interrupters—those who are interrupting unintentionally with loud whispering or cell phone conversations, and those who fully intend to make their voices heard, in either a supportive or an unfriendly way—overenthusiastic contributors who just can't wait for question time, or people with a particular ax to grind. The latter are by far the most challenging for any presenter to deal with.

Stay Calm

Don't ever get angry or try to argue back—this is a presentation, not a debate, so don't be provoked. Instead, try the following;

- With whisperers/phone users, it may be enough to fall silent until they realize you are waiting for them to finish. You can do this with a smile. Self-consciousness on their part should ensure rapt attention thereafter.

Choose Your Tactics

HIGH IMPACT

- Making the audience laugh about a heckle
- Isolating the heckler from the rest of the audience
- Insisting the question come later, and firmly moving on

NEGATIVE IMPACT

- Getting into an argument with the heckler
- Being rude or overly confrontational
- Trying to ignore the heckler— and failing

TIP **Ask anyone with a question to give their name, their department, and company, as relevant. Don't take questions from the anonymous.**

- With deliberate interruptions, firmly, but in a friendly way, point out that this is your presentation. One light-hearted way of doing this is pointedly to check the agenda and confirm that you, not they, are due to speak. This highlights the selfish behavior of attention seekers, but in a nonaggressive way.

> **Questions are an audience's contribution to any presentation**

- Point out that you are not chairing a debate. Offer to discuss the subject with the questioner later.

- With genuinely aggressive or difficult customers, get help. Ask a friendly face in the audience—or even the entire audience, if you are confident of the response—if they feel the same way as the heckler. Hecklers are relying on being one of a crowd, singling you out as the target. By appealing to the audience you turn this around, and they become the target who is wasting the time of the crowd.

Deal with Difficult Questions

Every speaker's nightmare is a heckler with their finger on the pulse; the one who asks the big question and puts you on the spot. Don't panic about this. Even if there is a hard question, you don't necessarily have to answer it—and even if you have the answer, it doesn't mean that this is the right place to give it. If there is a crucial question that you are afraid of, think about who would be best placed to answer it and what would be the best situation in which to do so: it's unlikely to be in the middle of your presentation. Then, if the question is asked, you can agree to help to find that person and perhaps to arrange a meeting.

Take-Aways

The presentation is over. But was it a success? In some cases, such as a sales pitch, you will find out in the days to come. In others, you have no way of judging unless you set some criteria and find out if they were met.

Get Feedback

The key feedback you are looking for—known to the professionals as "take-aways"—relates to how you fared, and how you can improve your material and delivery. At the very least, this should involve asking your colleagues and friends, "How did I do?". The catch is that those you are most likely to ask are also those who are most likely to say what you want to hear. To get the full picture, you are going to have to go back to your audience and not only ask them what they thought, but find out if they retained the key message you wanted to get across. One way to do

Ask the Right Questions

A lot of presentations include a feedback questionnaire, which is usually left on each seat for participants to complete and submit. The value of these depends on the thought put into the questions.

At their simplest, these may invite the audience to rate content, presentation, or enjoyment on a scale.

→ Check boxes or yes/no answers don't demand much thought, so if there was an element of the presentation that was particularly important, phrase a specific question that can't be answered "yes" or "no," and invite a considered answer.

→ Make the effort to get proper feedback (and be seen to do so) by sending an email quiz some time later, to find out what people remembered in the longer term.

Make Contacts Over Coffee The post-presentation gathering can offer good opportunities for networking, as well as for getting feedback on your performance.

this is to seek out participants after the presentation and talk to them about their impressions. This is an easy way to get anecdotal feedback, but it isn't very thorough if you really want to know what people remembered of what you told them; you may want to use questionnaires instead.

Bite the Bullet

It's only natural to head straight for a friendly corner after a presentation, but the best result will come from doing exactly the opposite. Going over directly and talking to the hecklers and to those who dozed off while you were presenting shows your commitment to the task, and offers a second chance to win them over to your views.

TIP **The chances of having your questionnaires answered will soar if you offer a prize or reward of some kind to those who take part.**

Make a Graceful Exit

The presentation isn't done just because you've reached the end of the slides, summed up, and said thank you. To leave a really good impression behind you, there are a few more things you can do.

Follow Up Afterward

Answer questions that came up. If you've told a questioner you will deal with their point later, go and find them. Don't be tempted to leave without speaking to them.

The final stage of the presentation is the one the audience remembers

Answer questions that have yet to come up. It's possible to give an inspiring presentation and then ruin the entire effect by striding off when members of the audience are trying to reach you to ask more (or even tell you how good you were). Don't behave like a diva—make yourself easily available and you will win more fans.

Underline your efforts at tailoring. Did you incorporate the concerns of key individuals? Then single them out again, and ask if you accurately reflected their concerns and answered their questions. This emphasizes that you

think SMART

!

If you have a prior appointment, but don't want to rush off rudely right after your presentation, think ahead and set up a way to leave gracefully.

- Tell the organizer that you will have only 40 minutes to spare, and ask them to line up a couple of people to talk to.
- Also ask the organizer to make sure you leave on time.
- Those asked specially to talk to you will feel like VIPs, and if you're ushered off by the organizer, it seems less of a let-down for those who didn't get to speak to you.

> **There are always three speeches, for every one you actually gave. The one you practiced, the one you gave, and the one you wish you gave.**
>
> Dale Carnegie

were careful to gauge your audience response, and may also give you invaluable material for next time.

Stay for lunch. If there's a lunch, coffee break, or cocktail session after your presentation, don't skip it in favor of the comfortable company of your friends: stay and circulate among the people you don't know. As your audience relaxes in the more informal surroundings, they are more likely to come up to you and talk, and are also more likely to be positive. This is a great time to bolster your image with your audience.

Think about the Next Time

Even if you just wanted it all to be over, face up to the fact that there will inevitably be another presentation: only very rarely will your first presentation be your last! Don't switch off, or ignore problems and feedback because you have promised yourself "never again." If things didn't go as planned, think positively about how you can improve, and how you will make them better at your next presentation.

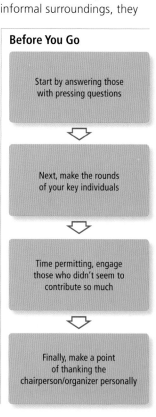

Before You Go

Start by answering those with pressing questions

⬇

Next, make the rounds of your key individuals

⬇

Time permitting, engage those who didn't seem to contribute so much

⬇

Finally, make a point of thanking the chairperson/organizer personally

Index

ad-libs, preparation 62
anecdotes 35, 103
animations, adding 94, 95
audience 99–117
    addressing fears 25
    background research 26–9
    contacting 100
    friends and family 51
    interaction with 48, 100–1, 104–11
    mood reading 100–1
    pictures of 91, 97
    role recognition 16–17, 19, 102–3
    tailoring to 21, 27, 96–7, 100, 104, 116–17
    who?, what?, and why? 16–21, 24
authority, perceived 103

background research 26–9
background of slides, creation 91
benefits assessment 14
body language
    using 65, 66–7
    walking tall 68

celebrity gossip 43, 103
cell phones, interruptions 63, 112
chain hotels 23
chart axes, clarity 90
checklists
    coding presentations 36, 37
    locations 22
clarity
    chart axes 90
    maintaining 60
    structure 36
    timing 49
clip art 91
clothing
    costume change 57
    dress to impress 54–7
coding presentations 36, 37
colleagues
    borrowing presentations 20, 21
    consulting 26, 29
    fear elimination 61
    guest stars 76–7, 95, 103, 108
    involving 43, 61, 63
    as props 76–7
    rehearsals 51
    video 95
color of text 89
colored checklists 36, 37
conclusion, memorable 36, 44–5
confidence
    changing location 23
    last-minute routines 59

content of presentations 30–51
copyright
    clip art 91
    music/video 95

examples, giving 42, 43
exits, graceful 116–17

familiarity, location 22
fears
    addressing 25
    elimination 61
    rationalization 58
    taking questions 109
feedback, getting 51, 114–15
filmed presentations, clothing 57
financial benefits 14
flip charts, using 80–1
focused presentations 32–3
font choice 89

Gates, Bill 62
goals
    setting 14, 15
    specific 15
greed, addressing 25
guest stars 76–7, 95, 103, 108

handouts, using 106–7
hecklers
    feedback from 115
    handling 112–13
honesty, taking questions 108–9
humor, using 34–5, 38, 103, 105

impact
    clothing 55
    conclusion 44
    flip charts 81
    focused presentations 32
    handling hecklers 112
    last-minute preparation 59
    podiums 65
incentives, offering 24
interest building 24
Internet See websites
introduction
    opening bang 36, 38–9, 44–5
    reason to listen 40
    rehearsal 17
    what's in it for me? 41

key points
    humor 34
    selection 33
    structure 36
    summary 36, 45

lapel/radio microphones 70, 71
lateral thinking 16
length of presentation 32–3
Lighthouse Technique 69
location 22–3

Mencken, H. L. 35
message
  appropriate 55
  avoiding presentations 15
  length 89
microphones, using 70–1
mission statements 17
motivational talks, humor 35
movement, working the room 68

naturalness, language 33
Negroponte, Nicholas 105
nerves
  co-presenters 77
  dealing with 58–61
noise, unwanted 63

originality 18–19

pace, sustaining 42–3
personalizing presentations 42, 96–7
pictures 90–1
  animations 94, 95
  of audience 91, 97
  clip art 91
  flip charts 80
pie charts, words on 90
podiums
  microphones 70
  pros and cons 64–5
pointers, using 85
positive thinking 14–15
PowerPoint 82, 86–93
  adding sound 94
  adding video 95
  blacking out the screen 97
  handouts 106
  hidden slides 97
  USB memory keys 96
preparation 12–29
  flip charts 80
  problems anticipation 62–3
  taking questions 108, 109
problems, anticipation 62–3
Professional Association of Dive
  Instructors (PADI) 49
projectors, using 82–3
props
  timing practice 48
  using 75–97

questionnaires, feedback 114, 115
questions
  follow-up 116
  handling hecklers 113
  questioner identification 113
  starting with 39
  taking 108–9

"ransom note" style 89
rationalization of fears 58
rehearsal
  body language 66–7
  fear elimination 61
  introduction 17
  perfecting presentations 50–1
  personalizing presentations 97
  projectors and slides 82
  statement checking 43
  taking questions 109
  timing 48
  whiteboard use 78
relevance of presentation 24–5
research
  background 26–9
  contacting attendees 100
  inside information 17
  location 22–3
rhetorical effects 89
role play 16, 104
roles, recognition 16–17, 19, 102–3
routines, last-minute 59, 61

satisfaction, in performance 14
sentences, length 33
shock tactics 38–9
slides
  hidden 97
  using 82–3, 86–91, 94
smiling 66
"so what?" factor 27
sounds
  adding 94–5
  unwanted 63
specialists
  finding 29
  props 77
spellcheckers, using 88, 89
stagecraft, practicing 64–5
stand microphones 70–1
structure of presentations 36–7
  journeying 40

take-aways 114–15
technical problems 62
timing, checking 48–9
trade titles 29

USB memory keys 96

video
  adding 94, 95
  of yourself 50, 51
viewpoints, understanding 16

websites
  information source 28
  inside information 17
whiteboards, using 78–9
working the room 68–9

Picture Credits

The publisher would like to thank the following for their kind permission to reproduce their photographs: Abbreviations key : (l) = left, (c) = center, (r) = right, (t) = top, (b) = below, (cl) = center left, (cr) = center right.

1: Real Life/The Image Bank/Getty (l), Adrian Turner (c), Adrian Turner (r); **2:** P. Winbladh/zefa/Corbis; **3:** Adrian Turner (t), Adrian Turner (c), BananaStock/PunchStock (b); **5:** Anne Rippy/Iconica/Getty; **7:** Yellow Dog Productions/The Image Bank/Getty; **8:** Gerhard Steiner/Corbis (l), Masterfile (cl), Adrian Turner (cr), Photodisc/Getty (r); **13:** Take 2 Productions/Ken Kaminesky/Corbis; **18:** Gerhard Steiner/Corbis; **23:** Jean Louis Batt/Getty; **29:** Strauss/Curtis/Corbis; **31-37:** Adrian Turner; **41:** Alyx Kellington/Photolibrary.com; **46:** Richard Schultz/Taxi/Getty; **49-50:** Adrian Turner; **53:** Chris Hondros/Getty; **56:** Adrian Turner; **60:** Ronnie Kaufman/Corbis; **67:** Adrian Turner; **69:** Real Life/The Image Bank/Getty; **71:** Adrian Turner; **73:** Chris Hondros/Getty; **99:** Jose Luis Pelaez, Inc./Corbis; **102:** Masterfile; **107:** Comstock/Punchstock; **111:** Real Life/The Image Bank/Getty; **115:** Image100/Alamy.

All other images © Dorling Kindersley.

For further information see www.dkimages.com

Author's Biography

STEVE SHIPSIDE is a writer and consultant specializing in business and communications. Steve has written extensively on these subjects for newspapers including *The Guardian*, *The Times*, and *The Telegraph*, and has authored several books, including *E-Marketing* (Capstone Express, 2001) and *Podcasting* (Infinite Ideas, 2005). Steve was a presenter on Blue Chip, a business and technology program on Sky TV in the UK.